To my Mum
Marie–Louise Aarts Bellefroid

You taught me everything about unconditional and never-ending love.
It was always there.
I love you.

"Once you realise that all comes from within, that the world in which you live is not projected onto you, but by you, your fear comes to an end."
Nisargadatta Maharaj

CONTENTS

	Acknowledgments	i
	Introduction	Pg 1
1	Harmony And Conflict	Pg 11
2	The Beginning Of Magic	Pg 20
3	Longing For	Pg 30
4	A Place Of Belonging	Pg 41
5	Inner Intelligence	Pg 51
6	Connective Consciousness	Pg 63
7	Your Authentic Power	Pg 76
8	Alchemy Made Easy	Pg 89
	About Leon	Pg 104

ACKNOWLEDGMENTS

I want to acknowledge everyone who has shared the journey and all those who provided a learning opportunity along the way.

1 INTRODUCTION

Inside Out: what does it mean? How do you do it? In a way it is very simple: it is the process to fully become yourself again, not hindered by past constraints, future fears or the illusion of limited resources. Imagine living life where you can just be you. Doing what you love, living in peace and harmony with everything around you, living in a world where everyone is happy.

Utopia? Not possible? I dare you to defy that. I truly believe that peace, happiness, truth, love, success, joy and all the other wonderful emotions and experiences we strive for are within us. We can achieve them when we have found our inner peace. The outside world is a reflection of the inside world, not the other way around. When we have transformed our own souls, the world we thought we lived in will look totally different just by our own transformation alone.

> "The world you see has nothing to do with reality."
> A Course in Miracles

In Inside Out, you will take this transformation, step-by-step, to open your heart again and get back to the gold which you truly are. This is possible for each and every one of you. When you recognise your journey, see where you are at, and why certain challenges are showing up in your life, you are already on your way to making the right changes.

It is often difficult to stop just for a brief moment, or even to slow down and think about what is actually going on during the trials and tribulations that your life throws at you. You may ask why these are showing up in your life and sometimes occurring over and over again. We all have moments that we think: "Is this it? Surely there should be more?"

How do you find an answer to these questions within your busy life with all the duties and challenges you have to undertake? What would the impact be on your life if you started to understand the deeper meaning of what it is really all about?

There is no reset button or option to start again. We are in this busy life and we'll have to deal with everything which comes our way. How do you decipher what is important, and what is real?

"To awake your heart is not easy but it is the only way."

"Who am I?" and "Why am I here?" are the two most asked questions of our time. What has happened is that in our culture we have forgotten who we truly are, and over the years we have started to live a life which we thought would be better for us. On our quest to better our lives we have accumulated ever more possessions. But has that really brought us what we are all looking for?

This quest, or dream we live in has caused us to close our hearts. Young children really live from their heart, and they show up in that way, yet we as adults teach them that adult life will be different, that they have to become responsible, and lose their childlike manner. We tell our children to become lawyers or plumbers instead of doing something they really want and love to do. Generally we tell them to become something they are not. Think about that in your own life: how often you were told off, or that you couldn't do something for whatever reason or limited belief someone was projecting on you?

Every time that happens, we instil a little voice in someone's head with a result that you create a pattern of behaviours or limiting beliefs, which eventually will hold them back. Eventually these patterns, beliefs and behaviours become a huge burden. There are many books written about this. In Inside Out we focus on how you can transform yourself, as all is already within you and how to progress on your transformational journey.

In my experience we are all born with a heart filled with beautiful love I believe that slowly through the events which happen in our lives we close our hearts. When you close your heart, you close yourself off from who you truly are. Your heart gets hurt or broken in your life. We don't want other people to see our broken heart, we don't want to show that it is damaged, what happens is that we build walls around ourselves so other people can't see the hurt. These same walls also stop the beauty, skills, creativity, love and everything we have inside ourselves to be shown to the outside world.

In order to protect our hearts we have boxed it in. The real challenge for you is to open your heart, to take it out of the so-called protective box. Only when you fully open your heart can you be who you truly are, live the life you want and be the best partner, parent, friend, family member, employee or boss you can imagine. The answers for everything in life lie on the inside of each and every one of us.

The outside world is a reflection of the inside world and never the other way around. Our material world can never satisfy our inner world. In our culture we have told ourselves that it does, that we need an ever more materialistic world. That is the reason why we look to have ever more all the time, and more and more people are experiencing the feeling now: "Is this really it? Is this all there is?"

I always imagine that before we were born we were sat behind a pottery wheel to create our own heart. Of course we each made a beautiful heart and were very proud. All of us thought our heart was the most beautiful of them all, and it is. Unfortunately, not long after we are born our hearts get hurt, broken or damaged because of the events happening in our lives.

Slowly we start to box our hearts in, building walls around it to protect it. No-one wants to be hurt or broken. We are shy and embarrassed and don't dare to show our vulnerability, show the world that our hearts are not perfect anymore. The walls you have built for protection, not to be hurt or damaged, are the same walls which prevent you showing others your beauty, your love and the beautiful heart which you made yourself.

Only by going through your vulnerability, those parts of yourself which you don't like to show openly or share, only by bringing them into the open can you find true joy, peace, happiness and fulfilment. That is who we truly are.

So let's go inside, your heart is the key and is the connection to everything around you. Only by fully opening your heart and living from your heart will you again become again that beautiful person you truly are. The journey, whether easy or hard, is about uncovering the layers, as you have everything within yourself. Going inside and uncovering the layers is about putting your heart out there in all its beauty. That really is all there is to it.

My story
In this book I will take you on a journey through my own story. I will tell you how I was in hiding most of my life and how through all the challenges and realisations I changed my life and opened my heart. Through seven steps in seven chapters, interwoven with many stories, I will show you and give you the courage to take the first step, how to keep walking and progressing to finally live totally and openly within your heart.

It is in all of you, you only need to rediscover and realign with the beauty and wisdom you already have inside yourself.

I have done many things in my life and in this book I will share with you how this gave me the insights into how you can all live a life with your heart fully open within the society and culture you live in. We look at how we have closed our hearts and more importantly how the changes we make inside affect the outside world.

We will use the wisdom of ancient teachers and modern insights for the transformational journey. Our ancestors and the old masters already knew there was a wisdom in the universe called consciousness we all have access to this which gives us understanding of how we can let go of the patterns and beliefs we have built around ourselves. We take it step-by-step, in seven chapters you will rediscover who you truly are and you will be re aligned with your inner core.

Everything I have done in my life I always did from my heart. A few years ago I saw the pattern to my challenges and my successes, and I promise you there were quite a few challenges; they made me to who I am today. It is all alchemy. Alchemy is about the transformation of your soul.

There is a pattern to the universe and everything is connected, that is even accepted by modern science nowadays. There is a pattern to our own transformation, and when you understand the process and what you have to go through, it will help you to make the right decisions and choices all the time.

> "If all the harps in the world were burned down, still inside the heart there will be hidden music playing."
> Rumi

About alchemy
At first it was believed that alchemy was the science of how to change lead into gold. It is the higher science of discovering the gold which we

already have within us. Alchemy is a higher art which needs to be understood in order to change anything. Scientists like Newton and Einstein spent a lot of their time studying the higher realms, and that allowed them to make their great discoveries as they understood the natural laws. In ancient times the knowledge of alchemy was kept from people as it was believed it wasn't good for them to know. Now, however, is the time that we share this knowledge with everyone.

In my younger years I was a top chef in the Netherlands. Cooking definitely is alchemy. From one substance you can make another which is totally different, we can change or add flavours to a dish or sauce for example. Yet in order to do that you need to understand some basic natural rules, and only when you master these you can start to play with them and change the cooking paradigm. This is what truly great chefs do.

Cooking is a great analogy to use in our lives. In every chapter I will use stories, recipes and my cheffing journey to explore and explain that particular stage of the transformational journey. You may have heard about mindfulness, inner peace, spirituality and consciousness. In this book we will use these terms as little as possible. What I have done is made an easy book where at every step you can see with examples where you are at and what you can do. Going within and opening your heart is an ongoing cycle of discovery, and the journey will become more beautiful as you progress through it. It will have its challenges, as we all have things to let go of. Once you start, there is no way back. You will want to keep travelling, to become who you really are. It is possible for each and every one of us; let's enjoy the journey. Do you have the courage?

I was the eldest of four in a loving family near Maastricht in the Netherlands, my parents ran their own business together and as with every child, I took some of my emotions, patterns and beliefs from them. When I was eight years old I had many friends and I was doing really well at school: never one of the best but just behind them.

One day when playing football, two of my best friends took turns in choosing their team. Now you must understand I couldn't play football for my life. My friends picked boys we didn't like before me, and at the time that hurt me. I couldn't understand how they would choose these boys over me. We were best friends! They just wanted to win the game, they didn't relate it to our friendship. I did!

That day as a young boy I made the conscious decision to prove that I could be number one in something one day, and subconsciously I was looking for that opportunity all the time. Being number one became my drive for most of my life. I am telling you all this in hindsight, as it is important that you start connecting the dots, recognising your patterns and drives in order to understand what happened. Go within and open your hearts for your transformational journey.

Every time when I found myself doing something new, that may have been a sport, a game or meeting new people, intuitively I made a decision, can I excel in this? If I thought I couldn't I wasn't bothered, yet if my inner guidance told me there was a chance I went with it with all my heart. Only a few years ago I finally managed to break this pattern, which was like a rebirth, a very important moment in my life and the further opening of my heart.

I have always been conscious about my weight. As a boy I was overweight, I was an emotional eater just like my mum, which made me feel insecure. As I kept telling myself that, I started the habit of eating even more, a result of feeling often that I wasn't good enough. Other emotions I took from my dad; he is from a wonderful working class family, the eldest of 9 children. When my dad was 23, married with one child and the second on the way, he wanted to start his own business and asked his parents for support. They didn't understand and advised him against it. My dad felt very disappointed and not supported by his own parents. He became very successful as a businessman, although the feeling stayed with him that he had to prove himself. As a young boy I subconsciously took on those feelings. For a long time I always felt that I had to do things on my own, a concept which has been very ingrained in our Western society and in our educational system, and that there was no support for me.

Illusions
Of course it was the illusion which I created myself. You can see in your own life how these situations create certain patterns and belief systems for each of us. Our parents and the people around us always give us the best possible advice, full of love, yet they may have been unaware that their heart was closed and they acted from their own perspective and belief systems. They meant well but weren't always helpful to us. In Inside Out we follow the path, learning how to recognise and let go of the patterns and beliefs. How can you become lighter and travel faster in this beautiful journey called life?

In life and in nature everything goes in cycles, that is how it works. As human beings we can also recognise the cycles and follow them as they are presented to us. There is always an order to it: winter, spring, summer and fall. Fall will never come before summer and so on. When you start to see the patterns and cycles in your life, you can see them for what they are, rather than being moved and drawn into them.

When you are able to recognise the pattern, and stay unmoved by it, and balanced within yourself, you will be able to react in the best possible way and move on. We often have the tendency to let our emotions and ego take the upper hand. Before we know it we are stuck again in our old patterns and beliefs, which seem so difficult to break.

> "It is only the individual possessed of supreme sincerity who can give full development to his nature. Able to give full development to his nature, he can give full development to the nature of all men."
> Lao Tzu

It is an ongoing cycle and as you keep undoing and growing it becomes easier. Steve Jobs said it so famously in his Stanford Commencement Speech: "We need to connect the dots yet we can only connect them backwards." I will share my story and you can see how I connected the dots backwards. As you will be connecting your own dots, the insights, realisations, revelations and breakthroughs will keep coming.

As you open your heart uncovering your patterns and the things which hold you back, you will find that you start to see the world around you in a different way. As you are rediscovering, unboxing and releasing, you will notice that the world looks different, feels different, and the right people and opportunities are coming along.

When I was 19, I was overweight and just loved to eat, which came from my emotional instability. Food was on my mind all the time yet I didn't even know how to boil an egg. After an unsuccessful stint at a technical college I started at Hotel Management College, as I wanted to learn about management and do something in music which was my passion at the time.

It all turned out differently. In that first year, I had to do a stage of 30 hours in a kitchen, which I was dreading and thought I wouldn't enjoy. My dad knew a head chef in a very good restaurant and the stage was arranged. I worked on Saturday mornings only for a few weeks as the chef reckoned Saturday evenings would be too hectic for me as a novice.

I remember going into the kitchen that first day being very nervous and having no clue what I had to do. There was something about the buzz and camaraderie in the kitchen which I loved immediately, I felt at home. At the end of the lunch service the chef asked me if I could come back in the evening, which I didn't expect; I had made a good impression. I said yes, as intuitively I knew I could excel at being a chef; I could be number one. I share this story with you as being a top chef in the years to come taught me so much about myself, and cooking is a great analogy for our lives and the transformational journey.

Cooking is also alchemy and I will use recipes, stories and examples from cookery to explain the different chapters of this book.

Becoming accepted

"Only by unboxing your heart can you become accepted."

We all look for acceptance, to be loved, appreciated, valued and sometimes just to be seen. As the outside world is a reflection of the inside world, others can only see us in the same way and at the same level as we see ourselves.

When for example we don't see ourselves to be worthy or good enough, that will be the reflection we believe we get back from others as well. Even if they tell us we are great, we don't hear it, as the voice within ourselves will find a reason that it is not true or can't be so. That is why it is so important to do the inner work, and work on yourselves; as we grow on the inside the outside world will change as a result, never the other way around.

Sometimes people say to me: I know that I don't love myself completely but I do love my children unconditionally. I always challenge that and say: you can't, I'm sorry. The answer most of the time is, no, I do love my children completely. So I say: when I tell you that I am going to give you hundred dollars and I don't have them, does that mean I can't give them? Of course not, they answer me. Well love is exactly the same, what you don't have you can't give. When you have your heart fully open you can give and receive fully.

Only by opening your heart can you become truly accepted for who you are.

Explore your personality
In the next seven chapters you are invited to explore your own personality as the journey of transformation is an ongoing one of exploration, motivation and self-management. As you will discover there is

a motivation, a moving force behind everything, and as you progress through the levels you discover that slowly more and more things are falling away being replaced by a beautiful and blissful kind of emptiness. Within this emptiness, also called Wu Wei, you will discover everything. It is what ancient masters strived for.

Our characters are formed by our life experiences and as a result of this some behaviours have to be learned, others have to be unlearned, let go of. It is most important during your transformational journey that you are true to yourself, do the best you can and have fun with it.

Sometimes you might need to take action, or you might choose non-action. It matters of course how we respond to each situation, that we do that from our inner core and not from our patterns or limited belief systems. Once we know and recognise our patterns, how we behave and react, we can adjust them accordingly.

Everything is energy, also your reactions and the patterns you have within yourselves. As you become more aware you may notice that the energies become lighter and freer. As a result you may experience that physical and emotional blocks begin to dissolve or clear. Techniques which were used by the ancients - rituals, meditations and yoga - were important tools designed to help with the flow of energy.

All these contribute to the wonderful art of personal transformation, and as energy gets unblocked it becomes available to use in the most wonderful ways. You will find that your demands and needs in the material world will be changing. You will no longer crave for certain things which in reality were only holding you back. Your life will become lighter, easier and in many ways simpler yet more beautiful, deeper and more meaningful, and you'll see everything from its wider and higher perspective. Good things will happen to you as if by magic. You will be better able to deal with negative aspects showing up in your life. You will find that less and less of these negative aspects will occur as you change.

My favourite quote:
"Something hit me very hard once, thinking about what one little man could do. Think of the Queen Mary — the whole ship goes by and then comes the rudder, and there's a tiny thing at the edge of the rudder called a trim tab.

It's a miniature rudder. Just moving the little trim tab builds a low pressure that pulls the rudder around. Takes almost no effort at all. So I said that the little individual can be a trim tab.

Society thinks it's going right by you, that it's left you altogether. But if you're doing dynamic things mentally, the fact is that you can just put your foot out like that and the whole big ship of state is going to go.
So I said, call me trim tab."
Buckminster Fuller

Just before I start the real story I want to thank you for buying my book. You'll find all the recipes and some special extra gifts for you at www.leon-aarts.com.

1 HARMONY AND CONFLICT

Our lives seem to consist of that constant balance between harmony and conflict, the constant tightrope we seem to walk between these two opposites. There is a rhythm to everything in life, to everything in nature. Night and day, the seasons, the tides, everything comes and goes again according to the natural rhythm we have tuned into. Knowing that we can't always be riding the high waves and that challenges will come our way no matter where we are on our transformational journey, we can decide how we deal with the challenges when they occur in our lives; most importantly we see them for what they truly are.

When we are balanced within we can also approach or deal with challenges from harmony, we don't have to be in conflict. Conflict is a choice you make.

Due to the character we have developed in our life, we each deal with situations in a different way. Others - the people around us - are mirrors and show you what you need to work on within, by their reflection of your own rejected or denied emotions.

This first stage of going inside is about your inherited patterns and beliefs, how you identify yourselves in the physical world. Most of these patterns were established between 0-7 years old. You may have fears of letting go, scarcity or poor boundaries.

You need to ask yourselves where they come from, and being aware is the first step of letting go and actually burning the excesses. In most cases we have overindulged on our limited beliefs as our ego kept telling us that that is the person we truly were. Don't forget your ego is there to serve you and is trying to keep you safe, it acts according to your belief systems and as a result you forget who you truly are and move away from your core.

On a physical level we became more and more attached to the material world and convinced ourselves that we need an overindulgence of food, possessions, wealth, clothes or anything else which took our fancy. This first stage is about letting go, burning off what we don't need. As everything is energy and energy works on every level, as you let go of a certain pattern you will see that it will also have an effect on other things in your life. The energy becomes lighter and dissolves similar issues which you might be attached to on a physical level.

"If you are irritated by every rub, how will your mirror be polished?"
Rumi

Becoming aware
The first step is to become aware of the patterns and limited beliefs, of that voice in your head, telling you what to do. Once you are aware, you can build on your awareness and start to recognise your pattern whenever it starts to act and interfere. In the beginning this will be really hard as your patterns are very strong and persistent. Be aware what happens when you find yourself in a certain situation when a pattern shows up. Even when you can't stop the process, awareness is key and slowly but surely you will be able to do something about it.

This first stage of alchemy is very much connected to the question: Who am I in the world? In our physical world we have connected that to our cultural and family background; as we grow older it becomes more attached to our jobs, our house, our cars and our clothes. However this is often a false sense of who we truly are and can be a big part of the challenge, of discovering our true selves and living from our core.

On a human level we see exactly the same thing, we have become greedy and overindulged on the material possessions we believe we needed in order to feel happy and whole. Look around you, has it really brought you that happiness you were looking for? In our quest for more we ended up with the world as it is now, in turmoil and very much out of balance, where there is a lot for a small percentage yet many people suffer and are left behind, also in our western world. Wealth is not about money at all, true wealth is everything you have left after you have lost all your money.

In the trials and tribulations we have on a planetary level, we have not just left people behind on the other site of the planet - people in our own society, within our own families feel very disconnected - we have lost our connection with each other.

Every one we meet offers us the opportunity to mirror our reflections back to us. This also goes for the state in which we currently find ourselves as a society, it reflects our collective inner state. As we are becoming aware, we can work on recognising the patterns.

In order to be aware of the patterns and beliefs, you have to elevate yourself above what is going on at the visual level. Imagine you are in a huge parking lot and you can't find your car because the only thing you can see are just cars, and you can't look past the cars right in front of you. The best solution, rather than aimlessly walking around is to look at the car park from a higher viewpoint, from a tower or a block of flats. Let's say you are on the 6th floor, from up there your car will be easy to spot. Spotting our own patterns is exactly the same, becoming aware, elevating yourself above the level of the problem, seeing what is going on and making the necessary changes.

When I was twelve years old and had just started secondary school I was very insecure about myself, I was searching for my identity. I was overweight and thought I wasn't good enough in anything I did. Remember I told myself to find something in which I could be number one. In my inner self I told myself I wasn't good enough, I became very conscious about my appearance and that was what was mirrored back to me in the outside world. In my new secondary school, with many new classmates, I felt that I wasn't very popular and the other children didn't like me. That was the outside world I had created, it became a pattern for me, and took a lot of convincing myself to change that in later years.

It didn't mean at all that my new classmates saw me like that, it was the reality I had created from the inside. Often it is only when we look back in later years that we can look at these patterns, recognise and change them.

Connecting the dots

When we look at most important occurrences in our lives and we are connecting the dots, we can only do this backwards. Connecting the dots is about those times in your life when something significant happens which shapes your unique story. We might think that the feelings we had as a young teenager were insignificant, other occasions like our first real job or graduating for our degree are more important. This is a wrong perception; on a universal or soul level there is absolutely no difference between small and big occasions in our lives. It is all energy: it might be energy that flows or energy which is blocked or stuck. What is right, however, is that when energy is relieved and combined with more energy it can become a very strong power. As an example, look to water and how it flows in a river.

> "Life is a series of natural and spontaneous changes. Don't resist them; that only creates sorrow. Let reality be reality. Let things flow naturally forward in whatever way they like."
> Lao Tzu

The first step in your transformational journey, harmony and conflict is connected to your root chakra, in alchemy it is the fire of creation, the creating of a liveable environment. All our experiences mould us, they shape our character. Some experiences become patterns other experiences bring us great joy and comfort.

I'll give you an example. The pattern I developed at a young age to become number one was in many ways holding me back and shaping me very much as a person. Later, when I was training as a chef, in my spare time at college it gave me the determination and drive I needed to become one of the best chefs in my country. During that journey of becoming a top chef there were lots of challenges and also many great moments of pleasure, achievement and happiness.

As a boy I always felt I didn't belong and was looking for my identity, I felt at home with friends who knew me well, where I felt accepted. In new groups, meeting new people, I always felt very insecure and unsure about myself. I felt that people didn't like me, that I wasn't good enough. Cheffing brought me a lot, which is why this chapter is called Harmony And Conflict. The two go together and yet are opposites on the same scale. There can be a fine line between them. Where does harmony end and conflict start? The same goes for hot and cold: what is cold for one might feel hot for another.

What I am saying is that we need to look at harmony and conflict in a different way, it comes from within and what we create. It is a choice we make based on the experiences we have in our life and the emotions and patterns we sub-consciously have attached to them. It is important that we look at this, the same thing which can bring us harmony might also bring us conflict, and there is a fine line between them. This happens when our perceptions are based on the outside world, for example when our happiness is based on the possessions we accumulate, on the perceived world we have built around ourselves.

Everything is within and you will only experience true harmony and happiness when built on your inner happiness, connected to your heart.

When I started out in my first restaurant it gave me a sense of belonging and I loved it. In this job I felt secure, I felt part of a group, something I often lacked in the outside world. My insecurities which pushed me to become number one in something helped me to become a really good chef and I moved quickly through the ranks. The same limited belief also made me feel uncomfortable in many situations so harmony and conflict are really close to each other.

After a year I left that first local restaurant to go and work in a castle with one Michelin Star, one of the best restaurants in the country. Another step outside my comfort zone, a step which I needed to take in my ambition to become a top chef. Within that year in the first restaurant I taught myself to run part of the kitchen on my own. There were only six chefs employed. In the castle it was completely different, a brigade of up to fifteen, the highest level of precise cooking and a demanding and international clientele. The chef worked to a high and exacting standard: vegetables had to be cut all exactly the same size, a piece of meat which wasn't cooked exactly right wouldn't be served. I worked here for another year and loved it.

I realised that what happens in these kitchens is that the chefs have a higher understanding of the products they are working with, and this knowledge allows them to create a higher kind of magic. The understanding of the ingredients used, and what happens to them when they are cooked in a certain way, allows really great food to be cooked. Without the higher understanding of the process behind it that is not possible.

It is the same in our daily lives. When we understand our patterns and see how and why we behave in certain situations, we can use that understanding to change ourselves and our behaviours.

The first step is burning down the excesses, this might be material or emotional beliefs we are holding on to. In life it is often like this, when we think that we can't get any lower or nothing more can be thrown at us, only then can we start to build ourselves up again.

It is important to do this step first; do it well as it may take some time as only an empty vessel can be filled. Even when we think we have done the necessary work, issues might pop up again and need to be released. Always be thankful for when this happens and, importantly, allow the space and time for this to happen.

Letting go is the most liberating act you can perform for more magic and peace to come into your life, and to live with your heart open.

In the Introduction I spoke about the heart we all crafted before we were born that became hurt so, we hide it, as we don't want to show our vulnerability to others. Only when we have our heart fully open, show our hearts and its cracks will we be able to start building it up again. We can only show all the beauty and wisdom we have within when we are fully open.

Your light shines through the cracks of your heart, the gold which you truly are.

"When the Japanese mend broken objects, they aggrandise the damage by filling the cracks with gold. They believe when something has suffered damage and has a history it becomes more beautiful."
Bill Mobayed

What we can learn from wolves?
How can you bring back the harmony in your life, turn around the conflict and get rid of the excesses? You need to recognise where you have gone wrong. The easiest way to explain this is through a story of what happened in Yellowstone National Park in the USA. It is one of the most prolific discoveries made in studies into the behaviour of animals and their surroundings, and the influence of humans.

Wolves had been absent in Yellowstone Park for 70 years before they were reintroduced in 1995. The reintroduction of the wolves gave birth to the re-emergence of many other life forms. Since wolves left Yellowstone, deer had taken over and their population became far too large as there were no natural enemies left. Much of the vegetation disappeared because of the deers' appetite, and reintroducing the wolves had the most remarkable affect. Not only did they kill some deer, it changed the behaviour of the deer. Because of the threat of wolves the deer started to avoid the lower planes and retracted more to higher ground; this gave space for regeneration of much of the park and valleys.

Trees started to grow larger, forests and many other plants came back. Birds started to move back in, as did foxes, badgers, rabbits and bears because of the larger amounts of berries left to forage. Interestingly, the behaviour of the rivers started to change as there was less corrosion. Now what does this mean for our own life? Think about it for a minute.

Have you, maybe sub-consciously, as a sweet-looking deer, eaten all the berries and subsequently let all the other animals retreat and move away out of your life? How can you live in more harmony with your surroundings so everything will flourish? When you are focused only on yourself, it might look good for a little while yet in this story you can see that the whole environment is worse off. This requires a close and honest look at your own life; this might not be easy, but you'll discover that with the right changes, your surroundings will start to change. Everybody will contribute and benefit from the reinstalled balance in your life. This is the way to bring conflict back to harmony.

Acceptance or denial?
Too often in life we find ourselves in conflict about the mental and emotional challenges we come across, and there is a path we can choose to restore the balance. You either choose acceptance of what is going on in your life or you can choose denial.

Either way there is a path which can lead to the same result. If you choose acceptance, affirm everyone and everything around you and extend your goodwill, send love, understanding and gratitude to the people and the situations in your life. Regardless of the circumstances or what is going on, as this can be challenging, embrace everything and you will begin to see and receive the changes.

You can decide to choose denial and see everything as an illusion, your perception, or a veil which is put on reality. As you start to uncover and take away the illusions, and the layers of the veil, you arrive at the same place as if you had chosen the totally different route of acceptance.

When you arrive at that place where everything is fallen away, then you are ready, because only an empty vessel can be filled.

How do we bring it back to harmony? Ram Dass offers a great way of viewing things which I love. It might take some practice. We perceive ourselves to be better than nature. We don't judge nature, we revel in its beauty because of all its purities and impurities.

"When you go out into the woods and you look at trees, you see all these different trees. And some of them are bent, and some of them are straight, and some of them are evergreens, and some of them are whatever. And you look at the tree and you allow it. You appreciate it. You see why it is the way it is. You sort of understand that it didn't

get enough light, and so it turned that way. And you don't get all emotional about it. You just allow it. You appreciate the tree.

The minute you get near humans, you lose all that. And you are constantly saying "You're too this, or I'm too this." That judging mind comes in. And so I practice turning people into trees. Which means appreciating them just the way they are."
Ram Dass

Look at your world around you, the people and your challenges in this way, it will definitely change your perception of everything around you. It is simply the energy we give to things.

Use your five senses
The first step to becoming aware and listening to your heart, to see what is really going on, is to do this simple exercise regularly. We all get distracted easily; a little voice in our head keeps talking to us. When you practice this exercise you will notice that when your senses are fully engaged, the voice in your head can't be there imposing its stories and beliefs.

In order to listen to your heart, you have to be able to quieten your mind by silencing the ego. Go for a walk in a park or somewhere quiet, and consciously notice everything around you which you see, hear, feel, touch and smell. Only notice your five senses and be aware of them. You will experience that the little voice talking to you can't be heard. In that conscious awareness there is no place or time for the voice of the ego which is silenced. Use all your senses and see what happens.

You may notice things you haven't noticed before. Smells become stronger, sounds more intense, you can even taste the air. You become more connected to the environment around you. Every time you do this exercise it will become easier and you will be able to apply the new-found quietness into your daily life.

Do it as often as you can so it becomes second nature, it is a good start to become more aware. Take time and find the stillness inside.

Food alchemy
When alchemy truly happens the result is bigger than the sum of its ingredients. In food there are some great flavour combinations which go well together. Here are a few examples:
Vanilla and cream
Chocolate and orange

Tomato and basil
Chicken and tarragon

When we follow a few simple rules the results will be amazing, as it will be in our own lives. We have to understand the basic laws of nature, when we understand these we can start to apply and play with them.

When I had my restaurant I used to make a delicious basic fish soup, it had only four ingredients. The whole recipe was based on the quality of the ingredients and a basic understanding of cooking and what happens when you combine ingredients. The skill was to know exactly when to add the next ingredient.

10 finely sliced shallots
1 bottle Nouilly Prat
750ml fish stock
750ml double cream

Sweat the shallots in a bit of olive oil without colouring until they are soft and cooked. Add the Nouilly Prat and reduce until a thick golden syrup is left. Add the fish stock and reduce by half. Then add the cream, bring to the boil and season.

That's all there is to it. You can use this recipe as a basic fish soup or reduced with some flavourings as a sauce for fish. Yet the same ingredients done in a different way can be disastrous.

Start looking at the patterns in your life, how you react, which beliefs are you holding onto. How do they return time after time in your life? How do you react? Take a clear and objective look into your heart, is it always open? Practice to become lighter, slowly unravel the veil and break down the walls, as transformation happens only with your heart open.

2 THE BEGINNING OF MAGIC

The previous chapter was about becoming more aware, recognising what is going on in your life, and finding that balance, a very important step. However this is only the beginning. Transformation is an ongoing process over a long period, and the deeper you delve inside, other patterns and beliefs you have taken on in the past will show up. However as you become lighter and more aware you will go through each of the different patterns faster and more easily.

Chapter 2 is about the next step in the journey of your transformation. It is about the further releasing of your ego. Your ego is strong-willed and tries to protect you and keep you safe. It responds to the limited beliefs, patterns and stories you have taken on and tell yourself all the time. It is important that you lose all attachment! As you lose the attachments you have, you will experience that you can go deeper within yourself. You will experience an opening of energy, which may feel like a real burst, and from this point onwards the magic of alchemy will happen.

As you are becoming more aware of yourself and the world around you, you realise that who you are in the world is changing.

For many years I thought that who I was depended on my success, in the way others see me. When you become a head chef in a restaurant at the highest level, your name is on the menu, possibly on the restaurant itself. The differences between the quality of the restaurants and the chefs are marginal, yet we chefs take our identity from it.

At the very least we have our names on our jackets, which are always crisp white. As a chef you take your identity from your reputation which is built on a few signature dishes. I might put a bit more red wine or butter in a certain sauce then another chef. Or I might pair two unusual ingredients which haven't been paired before; our identity as chefs came from those kind of details.

Who we are is not our job, the clothes we wear, our bank account or the number of holidays we can take every year. I realised this again only recently, that for many years my identity was built up from what people thought of me. Your true identity, comes from yourself, from the real core inside you. In 2007 when I was in Bali and I decided to give up my business - a story which I will share later - the decision was based on the fact that everyone thought that I was very successful. On the outside I was, I had been a top chef, I was running a successful fast-growing business, and I had two beautiful children. I realised during that event in Bali that that it was only the outside which people saw. On the inside I was unhappy: it wasn't who I truly was. What I had built up was all based on all the beliefs and patterns I had taken on during my life. I had forgotten and surpassed my true self, so during 2007 I realised I needed to put the balance back and that is what I did.

That self-realisation, acknowledging your true self is a big step. Realising, accepting and being truthful to yourself, where you are at, and what is going on in your life as I did is an important first step. At a certain point you become aware that there must be more to life than a daily pattern of eat-sleep-work, and a party in the weekend. Surely that is not what life is meant to be?

You might have had that lingering feeling inside you for a while, is this really it? From the point when you fully accept that your own self-image makes you who you are, the world around you changes.

The realisation that who you are in this world is changing, that when you let go of the self-preservation, and who you believe you are, and that when you step away from the personal survival route you are on, you can do all that when you truly become aware of everything you have been telling yourself. After the realisation it is important you become aware where everything you hold onto comes from, only at that deeper level you will have a better understanding.

Only when you really go to that deep understanding and know where it comes from will you be able to change your beliefs and patterns.

Bliss of wellbeing

The opening up of energy which happens when you open up on this level, opening your heart to an even greater extent, will be just amazing. You will be blown away and the feeling you'll experience will be something totally new. It is an indicator of things to come.

As you are breaking down the ego even further, there will be less in your way allowing you to go further down the path of who you truly are and removing the obstacles which were holding you back.

It is like popping your head above the clouds for the very first time, when a whole new world opens up to you, which is as exciting as something you have never experienced before. For the first time you notice that there is a beautiful landscape and the sun is shining and you realise it has been there all the time.

This blissful feeling and the renewed energy will show up in different ways. You might suddenly hear people say something which is exactly what you need to hear at that time. Old friends or contacts might come back into your life, seemingly out of the blue. Wonderful opportunities and offers appear just because you are becoming more aware.

Like energy seeks like energy, and that goes for every kind of energy. This is the point where you start looking at everything from a renewed perspective. Your view is less troubled by previous doubts and thoughts. This renewed experience of energy will allow you to become lighter, to see things in a different light and as you do that, opportunities and openings will come into your life as a result.

Personal survival

In order to achieve this changing state, to change from the person you thought you were, there are a few things to look at: your inner child and your buried emotions. Allow yourself to lose yourself in them fully. Make no mistake, this part of your transformation can and will be tough. You are facing some of your deepest, most rejected parts, you might need to loosen yourself from your family or other people close to you.

It is looking at what is held back. Intuitively and inherently we know what is holding us back. It might be that you have a very domineering and controlling mother and as a result now, even with having your own children and a very successful job, you don't know how to deal with a controlling colleague or boss. You might automatically fall back into the same pattern you have developed as a child. It could be that you retract whenever your mum started telling you what to do, how to behave and when to do your homework? Your solution might have been to be very quiet so she wouldn't notice you, or maybe you did everything she said as you felt that would keep the peace. As an adult you might be aware of this pattern, and every time a similar situation happens at work you can feel yourself slipping back, and you haven't got the power to change the reality, to come up for yourself and to change your behaviour.

Your colleagues might even wonder what is going on and don't understand why you don't participate at certain times. A pattern which was developed as a personal survival mechanism probably doesn't suit you in your current reality. In order to let go and change it requires you to go deep within and face some deep parts of the ego and mind.

We have created a reality where we thought we were someone based on gratification, validation and most of all control. The release of the wonderful energies and bliss comes from when we fully surrender and let go of all of these.

"When you identify with the limits of the body and take that as your reality, the anxiety and suffering exists. When you see who you truly are then you can enjoy the vast display of the universe as it dances it infinite dance."

Because of some of my own limited beliefs and patterns, as a child I thought that my family didn't really want me around during family dinners, watching TV together or just going out somewhere. My mind kept telling me this and it was the reality I created. With every single little thing which happened I would say to myself: You see, they don't want me here; they have fun, I don't.

I tried not to take part in family gatherings and retracted to my room often, convinced it was the best for all of us. I even found a whole group of separate friends. It was me, there was nothing wrong with my family and we grew up in a loving environment.

This pattern stayed with me and became a large part of who I thought I was even later in my life. When I was already a successful chef, I would often feel that I wasn't good enough and didn't belong around my peers, although they saw me as their equal. That little voice was always there in my head. You can understand my struggle of never feeling good enough.

I conquered this a few years ago, when I was on my transformational journey and a spiritual mentor I had at the time said: "Leon, you need to look at this, you have neglected your inner child." At the time I thought my life was going very well and I was really in flow. I knew there was a part of me which I neglected, I just thought I could keep that door shut, everything was going well, right? How wrong I was! His comment surprised me at first; the good thing about having a mentor is that they are always two steps ahead of you.

He continued: "What happens when you leave a child locked up in a room overnight and you open the door the next day? It will not come out spontaneously and happy. It will be afraid and wonder what will happen next." When we neglect a part of ourselves it will be exactly the same. You have to nurture that part of yourself, your inner child, and give it a lot of attention and love all the time, assuring it you are there.

Andrew and I spoke about my neglected part a bit more, and a few days later I had this wonderful dream in that space between being asleep and waking up. I saw myself at the age of about twelve lying on my bed, in my room, reading a book, pretending I wanted to be there and that I was happy. At the same time my whole family was in the living room, on the other side of the hall, having fun - there was some kind of party going on.

In this lucid dream I saw myself getting up; it felt as if I was leaving my body. I left my room and apprehensively went into the living room. To my surprise my family was happy to see me and welcomed me. They wanted me there. This was a huge insight and so different than the story I had told myself over and over again. It was only me who was living that story and created a whole belief system around it.

At the time of working with Andrew, we worked on my inner child and it was very hard at times. He showed me how the pattern I had created stopped me from becoming who I truly am and achieving my greatness. I also experienced that as soon as I started to focus and let go of the story, things around me changed almost overnight.

Buried emotions and your inner child

Our inner child tells us so much about ourselves, where we are now and who we truly are. I often ask people to tell me about their inner child. What would others see if they could truly see your inner child? Intuitively we always know how to tap into that, as our inner child will tell us. It is who you truly are, and your inner child wants to come out and play. As we might feel ashamed or embarrassed about certain things which happened to us when we were young, within our societies we have got used to burying these experiences which hurt or damaged us. We have become afraid to show our true selves and our vulnerability; we have built protective walls around ourselves. We don't let others see inside of us anymore, just so no-one can see that we are hurt, that our heart is broken. We bury all the waste we produce on our planet in huge landfills, because we think: It is a way we can't see it anymore. The question remains of course: did we really get rid of it or is it just hidden and out of sight? By burying anything we are not really solving the problem.

Waste or emotions: it is exactly the same. Look at the emotions you have buried deep inside yourself, what is it you don't want to look at? Within these emotions and the experiences you don't want to revisit, you'll find all the answers to free yourself.

By now you have heard that we are all made up of 100% light or love. Only 2% of our whole being ever gets hurt, broken or damaged. This also means that 98% of your whole being never gets broken, damaged or hurt. Maybe you are a worst case scenario, and this might mean that 95% of you is still fully intact, full of light and love. We spend most of our time thinking, worrying, pondering and procrastinating about that 5%, all the bad things which have happened to us.

A while ago, when speaking to a friend who couldn't let go of some family stuff, I said to her: You agree that 95% of you has never been hurt? She said yes, so I said to her, ok then you need to focus 57 minutes of every hour (95%) of the love and light which you are. The beauty which is inside you, the other 5%, 3 minutes you can spend on the hurt and the pain. That way both get equal attention. I promise you when you start looking at it that way and give even half the amount of time and attention to your beauty, greatness and wisdom, your life will change overnight, guaranteed!

Brene Brown famously talks about our vulnerability and how only by accepting and going through those vulnerable places will we be able to find true joy, happiness, pleasure, wealth and peace. It can be scary at first to go to these emotions, and your ego will try to stop you, but you will need to pass them in your transformational journey to become free and light. To become 100% you!

Food and emotions

Food is important to us in many ways: we need food to grow, to nurture, to energise us and simply to stay alive. Food can also nurture us on an emotional level. We all have certain meanings attached to different kinds of foods. For example, what you eat with your family traditionally at Easter or Christmas, a dish or cake your mum would make for your birthday or what she cooked when you felt sad.

Think about what we call comfort food, your favourite dishes, a hearty stew when the weather is really cold. Or even what happens around a table, when we come together to celebrate a birthday, a special occasion or just a family get-together. Great food and eating can bring people together, and hence the memories of these special occasions, happiness, bliss, fun and gratitude. We can also attach sadness, fear or anger to food and meals we have shared together as at a certain time something might have happened.

From solid to liquid
On an alchemical level, stage two is about bringing a substance from solid to liquid, after is has been brought back to its essence. It is changed into a liquid in order to change it back later into the required state, which of course is gold. A recipe which goes with this is a soup where we take beautiful ingredients at their prime and change their form while still preserving all the flavours.

Soup is also the ultimate comfort food. This is one of my all-time favourites which I served in my restaurants: Laksa, which can be served in a variety of ways. Feel free to take out or add ingredients to create your own magical recipe.

Serves 4-6

Laksa Paste
- 8 small dried red chillies
- 2 tbsp dried shrimps
- 5 red shallots chopped
- 1 tbsp finely chopped galangal
- 3 garlic cloves, chopped
- W large lemongrass stalks, trimmed and chopped
- 6 candle nuts chopped
- 2 tsp ground coriander
- 1 tsp ground cumin
- 1 tsp ground turmeric

Soup
- 1 dl vegetable oil
- 1.5 ltr chicken stock
- 21/2 tsp grated palm sugar
- 450 gr chicken thighs with bone and skin, or chicken thigh fillets thickly sliced

- 12 large raw king prawns, shelled, tails intact, intestinal tract removed
- 500 ml coconut milk
- 150 gr tofu puffs thickly sliced
- 200 gr bean sprouts
- 500 gr fresh tin rice noodles
- Fresh Asian shallots, mint leaves, chili sambal and lime wedges to serve

To make the laksa paste, place the chillies and shrimps in two separate bowls and pour over enough boiling water to cover both. Leave for 20 minutes or until softened. Drain well, then process with remaining ingredients in a food processor to a smooth paste.

Heat oil in a large saucepan over medium heat. Add the laksa paste and cook, stirring for 2 minutes or until fragrant. Add the stock and sugar. Stir to combine the ingredients, and bring to a simmer. Add the chicken, return to a simmer and cook for 4 minutes. Add the prawns and cook for 1 further minute or until chicken is cooked through and prawns are almost cooked.

Add the coconut milk, tofu, and beansprouts. Stir gently to combine, then bring almost to a simmer. Reduce to a low heat and cook for 2 minutes or until prawns are just cooked, beansprouts are wilted and tofu is heated through.

Meanwhile, place the noodles in a large bowl. Pour over enough boiling water to cover, then stand for 2 minutes or until heated through. Drain well. Divide the noodles in the serving bowls, add the laksa. Scatter over fried shallots and mint leaves. Spoon over chilli sambal, if desired, and serve immediately with lime wedges.

I have always been an emotional eater, just like my mum. I remember when I was young and she had a challenge in her life she would open the kitchen cupboard and grab something to eat, always with the sentence: At least I can still eat.

That is a form of emotional eating and I took this habit from my mum. For most of my life I thought I was happy as long as I could eat. I remember lying on my bed thinking that heaven was to eat whatever you wanted, you would never feel full up or put on weight. When I was emotional, feeling unhappy or sad I would just eat and thought that would take the feeling away. Of course it was just a quick fix.

My eating habits meant that I was overweight for a long time, the real cause was my emotional imbalance. Once I started to work on my emotional state the weight disappeared very easily. My emotions, not my weight, caused me to get diabetes, a story which I will share in the next chapter.

As I share these stories with you, you might look at your own life and recognise the patterns. At this stage take them to a deeper level of understanding and let go of the stories you have told yourself. Take some time for yourself, meditate on it, write them down, talk to some old friends or family and work on releasing them. I can't say it often enough; this stage is about the destruction of the ego.

Kitchens have historically always been run in a very hierarchical system, just like we had the mastery system in the Middle Ages. From becoming an apprentice to becoming master in what you do, there was a certain structure to it, making sure that all the aspects of becoming a master were covered during the process. As in alchemy, when you have gone through the whole process and understand the spiritual aspects lying behind everything, that is the moment that you will change.

Becoming a master in what you do is important as you will have total mastery over a subject, your profession or a field of interest. What happens is that you are so familiar with what you do, you can stretch time while you are doing it. If you and I were in the kitchen, where I have achieved mastery, because of my knowledge I can skip certain steps when preparing a recipe as many handlings have become second nature to me. I don't need to think about it; you on the other hand, do. What happens is that I will have more time to create something wonderful, watch and control the food as it cooks. So I stretch time and use my understanding to cook something magical. Of course in your field of mastery this will be the other way round. One of my mentors told me early in my career: "Leon, become a master in everything you do!" Genius is the next level of mastery.

"A master hits a target nobody else can, a genius hits a target no-one else can even see." Unknown

Classical kitchens are set up with several different sections, also known as a 'partie'. Each section prepares part of what is needed to cook the menu and dishes, for example, fish, pastry, vegetables, cold starters, sauce and meat. A chef running a section in the kitchen is called a chef de partie. As a young chef you enter the kitchen first as a commis; in this job you assist the chefs of your section, depending on the size of the brigade, there might even be a first, second and third commis and a demi chef de partie.

The whole system is built that over the course of a few years you go through every section to learn it, with the goal to become a chef de partie. When you have been a chef de partie for a couple of years, preferably running several sections you can become sous chef and maybe head chef. This path of learning your profession could take years and is often taken in several kitchens of different status and cookery style, so your experience is as wide as possible before reaching your mastery level.

Even as a head chef you keep learning and developing not just purely as a chef, but about the development of your recipes, staff management and people skills.

This classical system stemmed from the systems that were in place in the Middle Ages, and had been built upon over hundreds of years. During your training you often have a mentor, a person who would support you, track your progress, give advice and help you make a decision on where to go next. It wasn't just about learning your trade, it was about becoming a better person, more balanced and aware.

Going through the system teaches much understanding about who you are as a person, how other people are and where they are at in their life. Make no mistake, it was tough going through the whole system, not many who started in any field would make it to the highest level of achieving mastery.

The transformation of your soul, and the steps in understanding alchemy are really the same thing. When you start to approach your transformation this way, you will start to recognise the process which is involved. Looking at it already with the awareness you have of your own limited beliefs and patterns will help you to see what the necessary next steps for you will be.

3 LONGING FOR

Twelve years ago, in 2002, a few months before my daughter was born I was diagnosed with diabetes during a regular medical check-up. It came as an absolute shock to me. I thought I was living quite healthily, working hard to grow my business. Doctors generally step into fear immediately and warn you about all the consequences of your diet and your weight.

Intuitively I felt that something else was going on, the diabetes and even my weight was a result, not the cause, of my disease. After some research I discovered that diabetes often comes from a period of deep grief and it takes an average of about seven years to surface.

Seven years earlier, in 1995, my mother passed away very suddenly. She, together with my dad, my wife and I were running our restaurant. She was just 51, and you can imagine such a shock brought many complications for the family and the business. I was still trying to prove myself as a chef, and looking to be that number one, to excel. I was also still hosting many insecurities.

I was longing for something, I was longing to be accepted for who I truly was. I thought I had to find that place somewhere else, somewhere outside myself. At the time I truly believed that through the approval of others I would find that place. Peace within doesn't come from others, no one will see you for who you truly are if you can't see it yourself. My longing was very strong, I even go as far as saying it dictated my life.

My mum was extremely important to me, as for everyone. She had a beautiful energy, wisdom and presence. Our regular chats helped me to stay on my journey, stay focused, and her insights kept me developing as a spiritual being. When all of a sudden that was taken away, both my dad and I struggled and our relationship became very strained and difficult. We were both on our own journey and at the time I might not have seen what he needed.

It was as if we both spoke another language, everything I believed in seemed to have been taken away from me. The restaurant started to struggle and I had a hard time coming to terms with everything. I felt I failed in my attempts to prove myself and to be a top chef. The longing I had for so long seemed to disappear right in front of my eyes.

Of course that hadn't changed and now in hindsight I can see all the blessings in everything that happened in those turbulent years. The seed must have been sown, and seven years later I found out I had diabetes. I am lucky and am still only diet-controlled. The discovery allowed me to look not only at what I eat but my fitness, both of which I improved. I looked deeply at myself and why I had certain patterns, and why I was searching for acknowledgement, fame and self-respect and even self-love on the outside. It was a journey which took me a few years and was very important in my own transformation. Sometimes we need these outside events which shake us to have a good look within.

Diabetes and many other diseases are on the rise in the world, and of course our eating habits and the way we look after our bodies are part of it. These habits come from parts within ourselves which we have neglected. In order to change we need to go on a conscious process and dig out formerly hidden material, decide what to keep and what to discard. In my life my deep fears and neglected emotions showed up as diabetes and this gave me the opportunity to dig deeper. I decided it was time to let go of my fear of not being worthy or good enough.

This third step in the transformational journey is about your personal power and self-esteem. It is about your own beliefs of your place within your family, your culture and in this world with friends and at work.

Seperatio
Alchemically this step is called seperatio which means to bring a material back to its purest form. Only when a material is as pure as possible can it best combine with other materials. On a physical or soul level this is exactly the same, here we need to decide what to keep and what to let go of. We need to become detached from the person we thought we were and maybe from people around us who don't have the right positive influence on us. This is something we need to overcome and it is part of the journey.

Take away and dissolve everything you are ashamed of; this is the uncovering of your heart. Take off the lid of the vessel you are most frightened off. We are afraid others might see what in our experience is not perfect. In doing so we have the opportunity to discover our true essence again in order to become who we truly are, in our purest form.

A practice which helps this process is a breathing exercise, preferably every day at a set time. Controlling and following the breath in your body will allow you to find balance and peace. It will also give a physical renewal and allow the soul to present to you what is needed for you most of the time.

Our personal power sits in our gut, our belly. You can often feel that when you are challenged or need to do something which takes an extraordinary amount of strength; you can feel that strength coming from your belly. Your intuition also resides there. It is the place where you combine the best of your heart and mind, where you balance between intuition and intellect.

"The wind is carried in its belly." The Emerald tablet

Your greatest strength can often also be your greatest weakness and the challenges or blocks you have to be aware of at this step are: fear of rejection, blame, judgement, lack of recognition and low energy. All of these are connected to your personal power. It might manifest in your life with regard to your self-respect, your integrity or you might be confused over the direction you have to take. My diabetes had to do with my self-respect.

There is another aspect: others show you what to work on with the reflection of your own rejected parts. It is what we call the mirror affect; people don't often like when it is mentioned, yet it is very important. That doesn't mean that everything you see in others is a rejected part of yourself, what you positively admire in others is also a part of yourself which is congruent and in its power.

"You can't expect to shine if you don't like to be dusted off regularly."

As a chef at the highest level you train for many years, learning all the basics and classics. Only when you fully master and understand cookery and it has become second nature can you start playing with the elements and create your own dishes.

After I did my training first at home and later in France and London, I went back to Holland to work as a sous chef in a very well-known establishment, an old castle. By that time I had a kind of classical training, I wasn't ready to lead a kitchen by myself, and I thought this place could teach me more about leading a brigade. Not long after I arrived the head chef left because of a dispute with the owner. That left me in charge with another chef, something I didn't anticipate and I had to learn on my feet.

I was ready, however, to create my own dishes, work on my repertoire, as we call it and it was a huge opportunity. Kasteel Wittem had been one of Holland's top restaurants for ages, most of the time with a Michelin star. The owner told me the cooking we were doing was the most exciting he had seen there; a big compliment. In the following years I improved and became known for my own creative style.

This creative instinct also comes from your belly, your gut, it combined the best of your intuition and intellect. It was that magic combination of my training and knowledge along with my natural instincts which I relied on during cooking and the planning of my menus.

When you have a restaurant outside of town, it will often mean that you are very busy at the weekend and quieter on weekdays, as we were. My creative powers often came into play on these quiet nights when our fridges were fairly empty and some other chefs or important guests would walk in unexpectedly. I remember clearly in these moments walking to the fridge, wondering what special I could pull off for them. I always wanted to surprise them and do something totally new and unexpected. Often I found that I was missing some ingredients for the dishes I wanted to cook.

In those moments, you often find a force of inspiration from somewhere unknown; I always produced my best food. These dishes would later become regulars on my menus. This occurred because in the kitchen I was in my personal creative power, very confident, and I combined my head and my heart, through my belly.

At times this was also my biggest challenge. When I was on a trip with other top chefs I felt never good enough, and felt I still had something to prove. Still a part of personal power wasn't healed, my self-esteem could be low which made me believe I wasn't good enough, showing me what I still had to work on. This is a pattern I have been working on ever since.

Refined personality

Before your heart really comes into play and you can start to make magic, it is important you reintegrate your refined personality into your life. The transformational journey is an ongoing one, a journey which will let you go deeper within all the time. It is not as easy as taking seven steps on a set of stairs; each step might take you a number of years. Some stages you will go through faster than others, and each pattern will have certain levels which you come across during the different stages in the process.

During this beautiful journey you will feel a renewed energy in your body, and your soul will come to life. The feeling of bliss, which is essentially your light increasing all the time, will never be gone even if you feel down one day. It is there just like the sun shines above the clouds all the time.

As you discover more of your true essence - the gold - it is paramount to integrate the lessons into your life. Life itself will show you, for example how you have decided to become kinder to everyone around you, from your family to a shopkeeper or a person on the train. You will notice that the people you encounter in your life will be friendlier towards you as well. That is just the nature of energy.

Your life changes simply because you are becoming lighter and are shifting patterns and habits. The right opportunities and people will show up in your life as a result, it is the way the universe works. Life attracts life! When I go to a tree, a living thing, I expect there will worms, insects, birds and other forms of life around it. It is just a fact. Yet when I go to something material, a car, which has no life in it, I don't expect there to be any living creatures attracted to it. Maybe only humans - you know what I mean. As you start to shine your light more and rediscover your essence, others will be attracted to you and show up in your life, even when you can't explain how.

At this stage you slowly start to reclaim the dream, which is you. You again start to believe that you can be fully yourself and live the life you really want to live from your heart. Inherently you know who you truly are and more and more of it will manifest in your life. Make sure you take the right actions, follow what your heart tells you, intuitively you will know and you will be freed from the restraints of your mind.

Aioli Garni

When we take the best quality ingredients, fresh from the garden, full of sun, and combine them there is hardly anything we need to do. Italian cooking especially is based on this concept.

One of my favourite dishes to share with family and friends in the summer when ingredients are at their peak is Aioli Garni, lightly poached cod with fresh garden vegetables and a garlic mayonnaise. Serve the fish in the middle of a large platter and lay all the other ingredients around it. Eat with healthy servings of the aioli and fresh crusty bread.

Make sure you only buy the best ingredients you can find for this and you'll have a feast. The difference will be immense when done with lesser quality ingredients.

For the aioli (garlic mayonnaise)
2 egg yolks
4 cloves of very fresh garlic, peeled
½ teaspoon coarse sea salt
7 dl extra virgin olive oil
Juice of 1 lemon

Serves 8-10

For the accompaniments (according to your preference):
Poached cod 2.5 - 3 kg piece in one
Blanched asparagus spears
Boiled eggs, little bit runny yolks
Haricots verts
Blanched broccoli florets
Peeled fava beans
Peeled baby carrots
Boiled new potatoes
Tomato wedges
Celery stalks
Fennel
Other vegetables to your liking, some raw, some lightly cooked
Black Olives
Crusty bread

For the aioli
Place the 4 cloves of garlic and the sea salt in a blender or food processor and pulse until diced small. With the motor running, add the 2 egg yolks and purée continuously while slowly drizzling in 2 cups of olive oil. Add the juice of 1 lemon and pulse again until thoroughly incorporated.

For the cod:

Turn the oven on to 180 degrees Celsius. Season the cod and put it one a large tray which holds it in one piece, pour a glace of white wine over the fish and cook it in the oven depending on size and thickness for 8-12 minutes. Cook it no more than 30 minutes before eating. The fish should still be a little warm.

What our cells teach us

Cells are the structural and functional units of all living organisms. Cell comes from Latin and means a room. Some organisms, such as bacteria, are unicellular, consisting of a single cell. Other organisms, such as humans, are multicellular, having many cells. Each cell is an amazing world unto itself: it can take in nutrients, convert these nutrients into energy, carry out specialised functions, and reproduce as necessary. Even more amazing is that each cell stores its own set of instructions for carrying out each of these activities.

When we are born we already have one hundred trillion cells in our body which are each a world on their own. Each cell knows what to do and does that function. It relies on the cells and the body around it to give it everything it needs and our body needs each cell to fulfil its function. So a cell is a structural and functional unit, which means that our organs like our liver or heart are also cells, even our body is a cell. Each human is a cell being part of our whole humanity.

As our body depends on each cell to do its specialised function in order for the body to be able to do what it needs to do, our humanity works exactly the same. Each person is a cell, a part of our humanity and for our humanity to function fully it needs each cell to fully take part.

By stepping into who you are you are able to fulfil the reason why you are here, your purpose. We inherently know what our purpose is, it is built into our DNA. It's your intuition, your power which will tell you what it is. Each acorn knows it will be a mighty oak tree and within the acorn is everything the acorn needs to become an oak tree. The acorn never has any doubt that one day it would be that mighty tree.

A human embryo also has everything within that it needs to fulfil its purpose on earth. Somewhere during our life we forgot and we started to follow another course. Just imagine you are reminded again, and realise you have everything within your power to be who you truly are and to fulfil your purpose here in this life.

Life attracts life as we discovered earlier in this book. Yet let us look at a mahogany tree growing in the Amazon rainforest, a huge, rare and protected species growing in some of the most abundant ecosystems on our planet. As this tree grows, full of life, giving to the ecosystem around it, the ecosystem also develops, and the more both play their part and fulfil their role the more life will be attracted and developed around it.

Your own life works exactly the same way: the more you open your heart, and become yourself, the more opportunities, happiness, joy, excitement and much more will come on your path, as it is attracted to your energy. You give back to each other and grow. Think for a minute how your life would look when that starts to happen.

One single mahogany tree in the Amazon has more insect species around it, than are found in the whole of the UK. The tree is fully in its own power, and the only thing it does, every day, is being a tree. As simple as that. Now imagine how you can step into your authentic power.

Heart work

We are now in step three of the process, and this is the point where you connect your mind and your heart, your intuition and your intellect. From the next chapter it will be all about the heart and the higher realms. The first step is to create a love affair with life, to fully love and enjoy every moment of your life, everything it brings to you. From the great positive and beautiful experiences to the more challenging ones, if you see an opportunity to learn and be grateful for each one, that will assist you to change your reality.

The magnetic field of our heart is 5,000 times stronger than that of our mind. Therefore, the state that you are in, and the energy which you radiate can and will be felt by everyone around you. When you enter a room, this energetic field will be in front of you and act as a kind of announcer for whoever is entering the room. We have all experienced other people's energetic field and felt their presence, and others will feel yours.

When you truly act from your inner power and have done the necessary work to stay in that power you will connect with your heart much easier. The heart work is much easier when you let yourself be guided by your intuition. You can train your intuition. What it means is listening to what is said from beyond the mind.

The challenge comes from trusting yourself enough to listen to your gut feeling, which is your intuition. Often, and particularly in the beginning, we still tend to listen more to our mind. The easiest way to stop that voice is to do the five senses exercise I mentioned earlier, or to find a meditation practice which suits you. Many people hesitate in meditating as they don't know where to start or believe they do it wrong.

There is no such thing at doing it wrong; what is right for you will be presented to you, it will come on your way. The most important thing is to feel that place of stillness within you as this is where you find all the answers and where your intuition will speak most to you.

The more you practice to listen and be still, the more you will be able to do it at any time, in any situation in your life.

"I have gained nothing from meditation. Let me tell you what I have lost: anger, anxiety, depression, insecurity, fear of old age and death."
Buddha

In my own life I try to listen to my intuition all the time and have been doing so since I was a lot younger. One clear recollection I have is when I was running my fine food business in London, we grew rapidly and in 2006 we were looking for a new unit which we could convert exactly to our own specification. Together with an advisor we made a business plan and approached several banks to get the necessary funding for our expansion. Everyone was very enthusiastic and said we would get the required loan easily. Of course banks work slowly, we had found a beautiful building which was just perfect, I had no doubt this was the one for us.

Time was running out as the landlord wanted me to sign the lease. I had a call on the 30th of March to sign the deal, the lease would go up by 20% from the first of April, and this was the beginning of their new financial year. An increase that high wasn't in our budget. I thought about what to do; the banks hadn't yet given me a decision.

My gut instinct told me very strongly that I should sign the lease. I signed on the 31st of March, without any security for the loan which would pay to convert the building. The first weekend of that April I gave the builders the assignment to start the work, still with no security, I just 'knew' it would be fine. As soon as I committed to what I believed was right, had acted on my intuition and followed through, the universe reacted and the bank signed off funding for us about five days later.

We were looking for an investment of 250,000, an amount my business couldn't carry on its own at the time. My intuition had never been stronger and didn't let me down. Earlier in my career, as a chef, I just knew when I had prepared a dish for a table, how the guests would react, if they would like it or not and what they would say. Without even seeing the guests at that particular table.

My intuition never failed me and I knew, but as a young chef I didn't understand it at all. Cooking is a very intuitive craft, skill or art depending how you look at it. An old mentor of mine, Cas Spijkers, once Holland's best chef, always said if you put a piece of meat in the oven, you'll have to go into the oven with that piece of meat. You will 'feel' when it is ready, there is more to it than just cooking times, advice which I still remember to this day.

Children are very good intuitively. Just the other day I said to my son, "Remember that on Saturday we need to go to that French course." His answer was, "You didn't remind me, I am doing something with my friends." I told him I did remind him the weekend before on our way to swimming. He disagreed and said, "I feel into it tonight before I go to bed and then I get a feeling if it is right or not. I always do that." The next morning he said to me: "What time are we leaving on Saturday?" I was so proud.

When you don't listen to your intuition, you will be out of sync with who you really are and your mind will take control of the situation. You will become controlling as your ego will tell you that it is the only way that the process or situation goes the way you want or need it to go, and you convince yourself it is the best way. It happens when you let go of trust, when you don't trust any longer that the best that possibly can happen will happen, when you let go of your inner knowing.

Think of a situation in your own life in which you are maybe a bit controlling, is it that you don't trust the other person to do what they need to do? In the last few years we saw a change in the way we work; more and more people are working from home. Employers traditionally are used to controlling the times we work and are quite fixed on that. Lots of research and experience has shown that employees working from home are more productive and happier, contrary to what was believed would happen.

Trust your intuition, as when you do you, inherently know what the right thing to do is. Long periods of control create habits and patterns and we have forgotten how important our soul and intuition, our true power, really are.

"The richer we have become materially, the poorer we have become morally and spiritually. We have learned to fly the air like birds and swim the sea like fish, but we have not learned the simple art of living together as brothers." Martin Luther King Jr.

Top kitchens are based on the medieval system of mastery, and cookery is an intuitive skill. The line between intuition and intuitive actions on one side, and control on the other, is very thin. The same chef who cooks based on his intuition, creating wonderful food being guided by that intuitive power often steps into force or control in the way he runs his kitchen. A chef takes great care to select the right employees on all levels to work with him, people often with extensive training. When it comes to preparing the dishes they have to show every ingredient and plate to the head chef before it is allowed to go into the restaurant. Whilst there is lots of trust in the chefs on one hand, there is much control in other aspects of running a kitchen, killing intuition and trust almost overnight. This is due to learned behaviour which is in our mind and ego.

We see this in society and it is important to trust your own instincts and power again in order to progress on your own transformational journey. Look at where in your own life you have created these patterns, and where you go against what you feel intuitively, look at these moments, be aware and try to listen and follow your intuition more and more every day.

4 A PLACE OF BELONGING

The fourth step of the transformational journey, the alchemical process, is about love and wisdom, the opening of your heart. When you have opened your heart wide enough you will start to see new possibilities to combine the internal and external worlds, the spirit and material worlds.

We are at the integration point between the denser energies (the first three steps) and the higher and lighter energies (the next three steps). The heart is about the union of your masculine and feminine energies, combining them together into a new belief system. A sense of knowing what to do, which is bigger than intuition, will become apparent.

The new emerging belief system will still need to be nurtured and you are discerning about what needs to be done. An open heart empowers your true self, bringing a new wholeness to you. This new-found wholeness is an important step to rediscovering who you truly are. There are new veils to be uncovered, more emotions to let go of, and you will discover what you need to do next.

The new-found bliss will give you the courage and energy to integrate this new wholeness into your life. The previous step was called seperatio, to make a material as pure as possible. This step is about creating a whole new substance out of the pure raw materials.

"The greatest act of courage is to be and own all that you are. Without apology, without excuses, and without any masks to cover the truth of who you truly are." Unknown

Connected emotions

With an open heart you are able to forgive; this is not possible when you are still hovering around in the lower densities or emotions. Forgiveness is a very powerful and healing process. It is not just about forgiving others: forgiving yourself is the most important aspect, as the higher energies and progression on your journey are not possible without forgiveness.

A heavy heart will hold the following emotions: resentment, anger, denied feelings and maybe guilt. A healthy heart will allow suppressed emotions to surface in order for them to heal. It is about falling in love with yourself again, and forgiving yourself, and that is the key to self-love.

As within, so without. This really is the key to inner alchemy. Everything you see on the outside world is a reflection of your inner world. So where you still find anger, resentment, hurt, or any of these kind of emotions towards others there are still unhealed parts within your own heart. Become aware of these, notice them and explore where they came from and realise they are holding you back, as forgiveness is necessary for the next stages of your journey and bliss.

> "If you're really listening, if you're awake to the poignant beauty and suffering of the world, your heart breaks regularly. In fact your heart is made to break; its purpose is to break open again and again so that it can hold ever more wonders."
> Andrew Harvey

Andrew Harvey talks about it so wonderfully in the quote above. We are so afraid that our heart gets broken that we protect it, we give ourselves a false sense of security. Only by going through the most vulnerable parts of our being, our existence, will we experience who we truly are and be able to free ourselves fully from the constraints we have inflicted on ourselves, our society and our culture.

When you are angry at someone for whatever reason, you are only affecting yourself. Anger, hurt and resentment are never the answer in any situation. When you discover what is still inside you that triggers these kind of emotions and reactions you can start to work on healing and forgiving yourself.

It might come from a birthday, for example, when you were a child and your father seemingly forgot. You felt angry towards him, you might have felt denied as a child. Recognise it within yourself, give yourself love. You are fine just as you are. When you do this healing well, the next time these emotions will not manifest again in a similar situation.

Only when you love yourself completely can you give this love to the world around you.

Love yourself
This is a very interesting part of the conundrum which is your transformation. A conundrum is a problem where you can't think your way out, you need to feel your way out. There is actually a rhythm to it, con means no, nun yes and drum rhythm. During the conundrum you will feel yourself switching between knowing and not knowing. You'll experience all the different emotions, it gets hot, it gets cold, you will be convinced you know and then at some stage doubt will step in.

When you know, you know. I can't express it in words, it is the most wonderful feeling and basically describes the alchemical journey you are on.

Self-love is an important step, it comes at this stage as the higher realms or energies will otherwise not be accessible for you. You can only love someone else to the same extent you love yourself. People often tell me: yes I know I don't love myself fully, I do however have unconditional love for my children. I always ask them: If I say I will give you 10 dollars and I don't have them, that means I can't give them. Sure they answer. Well love is exactly the same.

"Never ever apologise for who you truly are."

To love yourself unconditionally is not selfish either, only when you can accept yourself for who you truly are then you can accept and love others fully for who they are. See the good in everyone else as a mirror to yourself. Our whole culture and education system is built in another way. It shows us constantly where we are failing and should improve. What we still have to learn, where we are not the norm, whatever that means, rather than celebrating the uniqueness and beauty of each and every one of us.

It is so deeply ingrained in our system that too many of us struggle with it all the time. You know what I personally do? I always felt literally that I was good and not enough. Only recently I was working on this and realised in every situation I have been in, when I was successful as a chef or business man that is precisely how I felt all the time… Even when others kept telling me differently.

It is of key importance to show your vulnerability and go through these emotions in order to fully open your heart. When Jesus was portrayed hanging on the cross, that was exactly what it meant: he had his heart fully open. Even in those moments, the lesson he brought to the world was to have your heart fully open.

Spend time looking at the emotions you have which I mentioned earlier in this chapter. Become aware where you don't love yourself fully and why. When you love yourself fully for who you truly are, synchronicities begin to occur which confirm that you are on the right path.

A restructured inner self will emerge, the empowerment of your true self. This is the bliss which you will experience. It is who you are. Look at it this way, every ray of light has a personality. When we send white light through a prism, thousands of different coloured rays of light come out at the other end, each with a slightly different colour. This is their personality, kindness, wisdom, compassion, intelligence.

When you take one of these beams of light away and you send all the other beams back through the prism, you will not have white light coming out on the other side. So just radiate your light!

> "People usually consider walking on water or in thin air a miracle. But I think the real miracle is not to walk either on water or on thin air, but to walk on earth. Every day we are engaged in a miracle which we don't even recognize: a blue sky, white clouds, green leaves, and the black, curious eyes of a child - our own two eyes. All is a miracle."
> Thich Nhat Hanh

Union of the feminine and masculine
We all have a mixture of feminine and masculine energies within us. Everyone has a different mix. Feminine and masculine are different to our gender; most females will have predominantly feminine energies, some will have strong masculine energies and this might be strengthened by our culture which has been and is very dominantly masculine. For you as a person it is important to balance both energies within yourself and honour them. Both masculine and feminine energies have a certain role to play and are equally important.

In our society and on a world level we have suppressed the feminine energies due to fear. This manifested in a male-dominated society and belief system. Both males and females need to take responsibility for this as the true union of both energies will help us into a new belief system. On a personal level this is exactly the same.

The rise of the feminine has to do with embracing the qualities of compassion, interconnectedness and collaboration. There are things that men have to do in order to nourish their feminine self and things that women have to do in order to nourish their masculine self. This is due to real and perceived pressures from the outside world, where we tell ourselves things have to be a certain way. As our culture became more complex, we told ourselves we needed ever more, we were losing the balance within and the masculine energies started to take control.

"It is Western women who will save the world." The Dalai Lama

It is about balancing the energies within our bodies and bringing that to the outside world. When we, together as humanity, men and women alike, find the power and strength to balance feminine and masculine energies and accept these, this will be reflected in our outside world, which will come back into balance. .

All humans have struggled for centuries and our masculine energy often prohibited us from showing our emotions and true self. The rise of the feminine means that evolved humans will be shining examples to all children.

What does it mean to be an evolved human being? It means to stand up and live from your heart, to speak your truth, to accept yourself, to be able to show your emotions, to be proud of who you truly are, to find your life's purpose and live it. This is the challenge for men and women to support each other to achieve alignment of the feminine principle in a contemporary way. It is the conversation of the heart.

Bali's bliss
People often ask me if there is one specific moment which made the big change for me. Of course there isn't just one specific moment. However I always share this story because for me it was really the awakening, the moment where I said: "Stop." I realised that although my intuition was already very strong, and I had been doing a lot of work on self-love and forgiveness, a deeper 'knowing' had come over me which allowed me to have this experience which I now share with you. This knowing is very powerful and gives you the strength and courage to keep going even when the world around you tells you to do otherwise or thinks you are a fool.

It happened during an entrepreneurs business masters' programme in Bali, Entrepreneur Business School in 2007. Seven international mentors during an eight-day program transformed twelve business people from all over the world. At the time I was running my food wholesale company in London. We were very successful, it cost me a lot of energy to succeed as I always felt uncomfortable with the way we did business with each other generally. It's just about money. All my life I thought it was just me. Intuitively, it always felt 'wrong' to me, although it seemed to me that I was the only one.

During that week in Bali, I made a very conscious decision to stop and quit my business. I'd had enough. It was time for time for me to follow my path, who I truly am.

It was one of those courses where you had to present a plan, first they break it down, all controlled of course in order for you to come out better, clearer and wiser in the end. To build you up again. During the week I was asked a few times: Leon, tell us your story again! They loved it, that I had been a top chef from Holland who started a business out of nothing in London and now had some ideas to run an international social enterprise. This was not the way I took it. I was asked: Who are you? I started pondering, yes who am I? Everyone thought I was very successful, I could only see the challenges, which was all I could focus on. I realised I was very successful but that was only on the outside. It didn't make me happy.

Sure, I had a deep emotional drive to achieve everything but that came from my feeling that I was not good enough. Being asked who you are and the deep insights it gave me, made me decide to stop my wholesale business on my return to London. Not to sell it. We closed it. In just six short weeks. It was the best decision I've ever made. I was free. Now I could be truly me and not 'pretend' to be what the world wanted me to be. Potentially I said goodbye to a lot of money, I have never been money-driven, I was just so ready to stop as I realised it wasn't me.

The deep realisation was that, although I was successful on the outside, I was very unhappy on the inside. Of course the signs had been there for a while, which is why I experienced so many challenges. The universe was giving me all the signs. It wasn't my purpose anymore. I couldn't be part of a world which I didn't support and knew I needed to change.

> "Within each of us, there is a silence, a silence as vast as the universe and when we experience that silence we remember who we are."
> Gunilla Norris

On the plane back from Bali to London, I made the conscious decision to follow my heart. It was the longest flight ever due to delays but the result was that suddenly my life started flowing again. In the months after that, I rediscovered my innate purpose, started my charity and wrote a book. Only because I did the necessary work on myself, my heart opened and I gained that inner 'knowing.'

Global transformation

What does the state of our planet have to do with the opening of our personal hearts? Do you believe that there is a connection between the wars, destruction, the diseases and natural disasters we have on our planet right now and our collective well-being? I can't say it often enough: as within so without. Your personal experience is a reflection of your inner world; collectively the world you are living in is the collective state of your inner peace or unrest.

> "Hold a mirror to your heart what does it reflect? What will be the message of the legacy we've left?" Climbing PoeTree

The body is a microcosm and this is a reflection of the macrocosm, the universe around us, and the other way around. We have lost our connection with each other, we have forgotten that we are part of a bigger whole. In that process of closing our hearts we've became more self-focused. This is totally different to self-love. We became ego-centred, thinking that it was good for us to have more and others to have less.

Our culture and economy created this illusion, now as more and more people open their heart again and step into their greatness we have the opportunity to create the more beautiful world we all believe is possible. It is inevitable, we are all unique, we are all one and we have a purpose to serve collectively. When you become who you truly are there is no other way than to live the life of your purpose, the reason why you are here.

Each cell in our bodies has a purpose and it fulfils that purpose all the time. Cells are wired to do just that, each cell does 6 trillion things a second and by each cell doing what it needs to do, our body functions as the cells collaborate effortlessly.

> "The pollution of the planet is only an outward reflection of an inner physic pollution: millions of unconscious individuals not taking responsibility for their inner space."
> Eckhart Tolle

Our humanity functions exactly the same, we are 7 billion cells making up humanity. Each cell, each human being knows what role it needs play here on earth and we everything within ourselves to fulfil that role. Just like each acorn knows that it is going to be a mighty oak tree, each embryo knows what it's role is in this life.

Now just imagine what it would mean for our world if we all started living life purposefully, and free of past restraints. There are enough examples of what we can achieve when some of us come together and we truly connect from our hearts.

At the time of writing this chapter, July 2014, we are at the height of the conflict in the Gaza region between Israel and Palestinians, starting to blame one side or suggesting who should do what. We don't find a solution. Let's not forget human beings of all kinds are in the midst of these conflicts all the time. We are one family.

Rumi has put it beautifully: "Look at the sun. It gives its loves to everyone." We see the sun and it just shines, all the time. It doesn't say I give my love to one and not to another. In order for the sun to shine it has thousands of processes, combustion going on inside. To us it just shines.

Even when we feel the sun is not there, hidden by clouds it is still giving its light. Now imagine a love like that; could you do that?

I have spoken about the alchemy of food, how important the emotions are which we attach to food, and the memories we have with them. How a simple meal around a table can connect people, can heal and bring happiness and joy.

In 2008 during a trip with a group of social entrepreneurs to India we stayed in different places, from a five star hotel in New Delhi to villages of some of the most disadvantaged people in the middle of India. The best meal we came across on that trip was in a kitchen in Delhi of the local Midday Meal Programme. A fairly simple kitchen supplies tens of thousands of meals very day to schools all over Delhi to children who can't afford the meals. The charity is run by Hare Krishnas, each meal had five components and we all agreed that this was by far the best meal we had during those three weeks in India. This was all due to the simple fact that the employees prepared the food with love. Love for the children and love for the higher purpose they served. The charity was set out of love.

This proves again how important our emotions are, how we handle them and how they are transmitted into everything we do. It is energy even if we can't see it or when you try to say with a straight face: I am fine, really.

Masaru Emoto started a study in 1994 called 'Messages in water', in which he studied the vibrational and non-vibrational effects on water crystals with certain emotions. The results were almost unbelievable. His research has gone all over the world and the books are bestsellers. Frozen crystals of polluted water are totally different, for example, than crystals of pure pristine water which are really beautiful.

Remind yourself to have your heart fully open, love yourself unconditionally and let go of everything that restricted you to receive a new state of consciousness and bliss into your newly opened heart.

"Following our instinct or intuition is a better way of living life.
It is a gift to oneself to learn to listen to our inner truth, our intuitive voice." Don Jose Ruiz

Sauce Choron
When thinking about a recipe for this chapter, it took me a while. Remember this is about conjunction: creating a new substance from pure ingredients. Something the great chefs did decades ago when they came up with the sauces like mayonnaise and Béarnaise. Out of seemingly simple yet pure ingredients like butter, vinegar and eggs, something totally new was created. An ingredient like butter became totally different and fluffy when added to heated, whisked eggs, a real alchemical transformation.

Sauce Choron is a sauce based on Béarnaise with tomatoes added to them, it is a great accompaniment to salmon or grilled lobster. A dish I often served in my own restaurant called Lobster Marie-Louise, named after my mother. The real classics should never be messed with.

Ingredients for 6
- 1 dl white wine vinegar
- 1 dl white wine
- 5g crushed peppercorns
- ½ bunch of tarragon
- 3 shallots
- 250g butter
- 1 tbsp. olive oil
- 4 tomatoes
- 4 egg yolks
- Salt
- Lemon juice

Take the skin off the tomatoes by dipping them in boiling water for a few seconds, then deseed them and cut in small cubes. Cut the shallots in very small pieces. Take the leaves of the tarragon off the stalks and chop the leaves in fine strips.

Sweat half of the shallots in the olive oil on a low heat until soft, add the tomatoes and take off the heat.

Cut the butter in cubes and keep aside.

Put a pan on a moderate heat and add the vinegar, wine, the rest of the shallots, pepper, a bit of salt, and the tarragon branches, reduce until you have one-third of the liquid left. Sieve so you only have the liquid left and put the liquid into another pan on a moderate heat.

Add the egg yolks and give it a good whisk until you have a good very airy sabayon. Make sure the sauce doesn't get too hot and keep whisking, adding lots of air.

Taste the sauce, add the shallots, tomatoes, tarragon leaves, a little salt if necessary and bit of lemon juice. Serve. Enjoy!

5 INNER INTELLIGENCE

"If you bring forth what is within you, what you bring forth will save you. If you do not bring forth what is within you, what you do not bring forth will destroy you." The Gospel of Thomas.

This chapter, the next step of your journey, is about speaking your truth. The whole journey is about discovering your truth, now it is about bringing it forth, to share it with the world around you in the right way. Previously you have experienced letting go of the veil of thinking and being guided by your heart, the place where the divine reality exists. Now you have rediscovered your heart and its shell is melted, the light from your heart is now shining upon your mind and not the other way anymore.

It is from your heart where you are truly guided.

You are now able to discern between knowledge and real wisdom, between true and false. You are able to completely transform emotions into positive energies. This is a big step, stepping out of your old way of thinking and behaving into the new found reality. You have a right to speak, as the inner peace you are experiencing at this stage gives you power to speak.

Not everything we seek here will gives us peace. There is still reason to be cautious as some of the new-found freedom and insights will empower, and others might disempower you. This can be caused by loving and/or unloving imprints we still carry within us. At this stage some of the events which hurt or damaged us the most, especially with loved ones or about feeling loved/unloved, will become apparent.

My default setting was to prove to be number one in something; to my parents, to my friends and to my peers, whatever industry I was in. My limited belief was that I thought I wasn't good enough. By now, even with all the challenges within, I had discovered my purpose. Letting go of this pattern was a slow process, which I didn't recognise overnight as for me it had always been there. I didn't realise it came from not feeling good enough.

The active intelligence which you have acquired gives you a choice, it doesn't just give you the right to speak; it is your choice what you do with it. I was guided to stop my business and to follow my heart. That meant I had to become vocal about what stopped me, to share my truth and talk to others about it. I feel it is my duty. As we share where we are on our transformational journey we inspire others, with all those examples around us in order for ourselves to step up.

You will always encounter challenges on your journey: the true test is how you deal with them.

In 2008 when I had stopped my business and had finished a few consultancies, I decided it was time to follow my purpose. I just knew that I had to do it, something stronger than intuition calling me. In 2008, together with my mentors, I came up with a plan to sell organic food direct to consumers via monthly boxes. There would be several kind of boxes, and when you bought a box you would feed a child at the same time. It seemed logical, I had experience in the food industry, and a good third sense for sourcing great products. We were going to do business in a different way.

I started the business, bought stock and set up a website. Not long after that, I realised that it was not the way to really follow my purpose. My purpose is: No-one to bed hungry. It would mean again having to keep stock, find customers, have a warehouse and many other things. I had done this before. I needed to find a way which would be even more scalable, have a bigger impact and help end the hunger of children.

I stopped that business idea and started working on the concept of 'Fill the Cup'. It took me about a year to come up with the right concept. It was so simple and easy, it was exactly what I had been looking for. I had committed all my time and effort to come up with something which could have huge impact for hunger in the world.

I did a lot of research and came up with several ideas, and when an idea didn't fulfil one of my guidelines, I started again from scratch. In that year I gained a lot of knowledge, and a few events of synchronicity brought me to the concept of Fill the Cup as it is now. The concept had to be scalable, have huge impact, no bottlenecks and everybody should be able to take part.

In June 2009, a few days after Michael Jackson died, JP, a close and dear friend who lives in Los Angeles sent me a video of Michael Beckwith's Agape choir. As a remembrance and ode to Michael they recorded Man in the Mirror; it was really the first time I listened to the lyrics properly.

> "I'm starting with the man in the mirror, I'm asking him to change his ways, and no message could've been any clearer.
> If you wanna make the world a better place,
> take a look at yourself and then make that change!"
> Michael Jackson

I listened to that version over and over again; it changed my life. I had always wanted to change the world, and now I realised the only thing I could do was to change myself. Take a look in the mirror and make that change! I started to look at everything from a different perspective, and more synchronicities occurred. Two weeks later we were going on holiday to see my dad in Italy. Just before we left I quickly looked for a good book to read during the flight. I thought I would re-read The Alchemist by Paulo Coelho. A great book and easy to read, I remember clearly reading, "Everyone knows their purpose as a child and it comes back to you at some stage in your life. During your whole life you will be prepared to fulfil your purpose." That made me think deeply, I knew my purpose now, and I was also convinced I had everything to make it happen.

Not long after this flight I 'saw' exactly how I could help feeding millions of children. Imagine that every time when you buy a meal for yourself, you pay 25 cents extra and a child gets a meal in a school. You eat, they eat! I had been a chef, I had a food wholesale company, I had all the knowledge I needed to make it happen.

The structure was already there, it was so simple. I couldn't wait to come back from holiday and start creating it. We launched a few months later.

As I was developing and following my purpose, I was driven by some emotions still left in me. It had to be 'the best' idea, it had to be number one. Even though I was following my purpose and speaking my truth, I still had deep patterns governing what I was doing. Of course consciously I had no idea at the time.

It is important to know that as our journey of transformation is an ongoing one, patterns will re-emerge. You have to stay aware at every level; certain patterns can hold you back or give you a false view of what is going on. The mind and your ego are very strong. It was after the charity was up and running that I came to understand that some things were still holding it back. In my case, more than a year later, I broke the pattern of wanting to be number one.

Finding your voice and finding your truth can happen in a various ways and is different to all of us. Look around you, the signs are always there. Timing is essential. As human beings, we are very impatient. For the universe there is no time and we have to trust that the right things are given to us at the right time.

When I was developing Fill the Cup, it sometimes frustrated me that after initial agreements with prospective partners in growing our foundation, nothing would happen. It happened regularly. I was so passionate about making this happen. I learned the hard way that many people know with their head that they should do something for the world, but it will not happen when it doesn't come from the heart. I can write a book on that subject alone. Too many people act from their head, not their heart. Be aware of this, it could save you a lot of time.

The lesson I took from these experiences was that the purer I am, the more I will attract what serves my purpose. It is a mirror image, as within, so without. It will come to you in exactly the same measure. One year after starting Fill the Cup I was asked to go to Rome and talk to The UN World Food Programme in their head office.

"Only when you are genuine, honest and earnest will the wings of grace scrape away the dust from the mirror of your mind and reveal the secrets that lie in your heart."

The UN World Food Programme is the largest UN agency, and of course I was flattered that we were asked to present to them on our small initiative. I thought we could collaborate with them after 3-5 years. They already have many school feeding programmes and if we would work together we could really change child hunger for the better. They loved my concept and after a few months of talks we decided to work together. The World Food Programme made it very difficult for us; a big contract and all the responsibilities and work stayed with us. I found that difficult to understand, we were a group of willing, hardworking volunteers, why couldn't we collaborate more?

The collaboration stayed that way, with the World Food Programme making it very difficult for us to work and progress. I soon realised the World Food Programme was built on fear and lack. After 18 months, in one of our own board meetings, I suggested that we stop the collaboration. The whole board thought for a moment that I had gone mad, when I explained that there was no love and heart from their side into the partnership. The board agreed and we started procedures. I share this story to show you that, within the more beautiful world we all try to build, it is important that we surround ourselves with people and organisations who also act from their heart and have their heart open. Otherwise you will still be fighting the old paradigm, which is all lost energy; all we should focus on is building the new paradigm.

As you progress on your transformational journey you may find it increasingly difficult to connect with people or organisations who are not yet on this path. When the heads and hearts of all parties involved are heading in the same direction it will become very challenging after a while.

Discover your voice

"Silence is a source of great strength." Lao Tzu

With your new-found self you manifest what you truly want. The difference is that you now realise what is really important for you and your soul. You are now able to manifest what you truly want from within, what your soul desires to grow in this life and fulfil its purpose. It goes beyond the material. You have come to realise that no amount of material possession can ever create inner happiness.

The universe can give you everything you need, it is not just about manifesting, as that can also come from ego. What you truly need on a deeper level will only truly manifest when you do something for the common higher good, to serve the bigger whole. To be in service: that is the reason you are here.

When what you seek to manifest resonates with truth and is the honest desire from within, it will come to you in the most beautiful and wonderful ways. When you have found your real voice and have released the patterns and beliefs which you still hold within about love, this voice will reenergise you, reanimate and enlighten you on every level imaginable.

Your new-found voice will resonate with you so deeply that you will find a new vibration, and will know that this is what you have to bring to the world.

Finding your purpose
Your spoken truth emerges parallel to discovering your purpose. If you have absolutely no idea, you might have to go back to some of the earlier stages, revisit them and become aware of which patterns are holding the signs. Your purpose is not something which is just with you in this life, your purpose belongs to your soul and is part of the bigger plan, your role in the universe or on earth.

We all come to earth to fulfil our role; we have everything around us we need in order to fulfil that purpose. Coming into this stage of your transformation you have seen your way and you want to tell the world. It is about spreading your vision from your highest state of consciousness.

Your purpose has always been with you, and all your life you have been prepared to fulfil it. In connecting the dots, the challenge is that we don't always see the dots, we are too busy focusing on the road. Imagine that you are on a train journey. It always seems that the train travels the shortest straight line to your destination. As you are in the train you can't see or feel the whole track the train travels on. The reality is that it is not a straight track at all. Life is the same; we don't take enough distance to really look from above at the route we are taking. Only when you take enough distance can you see there were certain points were you took a left or right turn. These are the dots, looking at these dots you will become aware of the meaning of them and the direction you are meant to be going in life from the perspective of your soul.

> "People who are focused on their life mission draw opportunities. Their certainty of who they are and where they are going acts as a drawing card for others to align and assist. People love to be around those who are purposeful." John Demartini

In alchemy at this stage they talk about the peacock's tail. In the substance which a material alchemist tries to turn into gold, an array of colours becomes apparent. It reminded an early alchemist of a peacock's tail. When you come to this stage that will be exactly how it feels. A new richness and a variety of opportunities are present in your life. You will find that your life has taken a whole new turn, and many opportunities and synchronicities help you to take the right steps.

Purpose is central to an enlightened human life. Helen Keller wrote that happiness comes from fidelity to a worthy purpose. Pursuing a career, raising a family and creative vocations are all long-term goals for all cultures. Modern spiritual philosophy sees the purpose in life as improving the environment and world conditions for all beings. In the most immediate sense, this means each individual revealing special talents which are a gift to serve others. From a biological point of view, the purpose of evolution is the progression of genes. However, this is not necessarily the same thing as a human being's purpose, according to Dan Millman in his book. 'The life you were born to live'. He states that purpose is something that 'grows up in the universe'.

In Eastern philosophies, it is more a collective goal than an individual one. Buddhism seeks the highest level of joy; when you find your special talents and serve others, you will live a life of joy and highest happiness. You are in good company, just follow and live your purpose.

"If you have a sense of caring for others, you will manifest a kind of inner strength in spite of your own difficulties and problems."
Tenzin Gyatso, 14th Dalai Lama

When I truly discovered my own purpose I realised that my whole life had prepared me to live my purpose. I had been a chef, I had a restaurant, I had been a wholesaler and by now I had friends all over the world, all in different industries, able to help me. Often when we sit in our office that is not the way we see the world; it might look challenging and we have the impression that we need to do it all on our own.

In 2009 when I had the idea and a simple one page website, I called some friends in Maastricht, the Netherlands. "Why don't you start here, we know many people," they said. I went 3 weeks later and met Andre, a friend I gave cooking lessons to many years before. Immediately he offered his support to design the logo and website. Someone else who I only met briefly once before spoke to the local council and we were able to have a launch platform during an event in the local congress centre where lots of press attend.

Something powerful happens when you are in sync with your purpose and the universe conspires to help you. You will be so energised when you are resonating from the level of truly being yourself that you radiate that energy and other people can feel it, and get energised by it. It is as simple as that, you are lighting them up, and together you create miracles.

Understanding nature

"Act in such a way that peace arises within you."

By now you can see in all the steps we undertake that you are coming closer to your core, that place where there is absolutely nothing, yet where everything exists. All we see on the outside is an illusion. I'll discuss that later, as you know by now I love looking at nature and the lessons we can learn from it.

A tree just stands there, it stands still and in its stillness it achieves everything it needs to do, and so much more with a whole ecosystem around it. Buddha famously said that understanding a single flower would mean you understand life; a quote which had me thinking for some years, and there were times that I thought I did understand it.

Today I am wiser and I've learned that the more I progress on my journey, the more I understand this wonderful quote. Let me try and explain to you briefly what it means to me. A flower grows from nothing, and just takes whatever it needs from its surroundings to flourish, nothing more, nothing less. When the flower is ready and it opens, it gives its beauty to its surroundings, by just standing there. Not by shouting or seeking attention. The flower is just present. When the time comes the flower goes back to earth, giving everything back to where it came from in order for new life to come around. It is in total balance with the surroundings. How would your world change if you looked at yourself in that way?

"Be still like a mountain and flow like a river." Old Chinese proverb

Water is also a beautiful example. Water is shapeless and formless, it will always find its level. It can penetrate the hardest materials, it is soft, and can create the greatest force. As a human being when we can aim to be as calm as water on the inside we can also create this power internally. Not to destroy, but to overcome all the challenges we encounter on our path. As Bruce Lee put it: Be water, my friend!

The power of stillness

"Be still. Stillness reveals the secrets of eternity" Lao Tzu

Meditation, prayer, deep desire, a breakdown and transpersonal therapy can all help us to the mystical union which we are looking for, to achieve a new level of being after our heart has been opened. We find inspiration from something which is beyond us. Meditation is a great way of connecting with the higher realms, which are present in each of us.

In order to connect with our higher self and consciousness, we need to find that place of stillness inside of us. The stillness will help us to close off all the clutter from the outside and to hear what is really true for us. There are many ways of meditating; there is not one recommended method. The most important thing is to take the time for yourself on a regular basis. Just like every kind of exercise, you get better with practise. Intuitively you will be guided to what works best for you.

Give yourself the gift of silence and peace. As you do that and become better at it, you will be able to access your inner peace and wisdom in any situation and at any time, in an instant. You will receive inner guidance on how to deal with any situation.

In the stillness within you will find the answers to everything you need, guidance on everything in your life. Within is the real world, once you start practising you may find that you want to meditate more and it will give you peace and balance which, in my opinion, are key for the ongoing transformational journey. By now you have done enough inner work and have found enough peace to be still and quieten your mind's voice.

I meditate on average twice a day and everything I do now is because of the guidance I receive during these times of stillness. Sometimes I surround myself with light, at other times I ask a question. I know now that the answers always come to me in the best possible form. We discussed living in the moment and being present. Living in the moment is only possible when we have found enough stillness to quieten ourselves and to be present to everything which shows up.

Set yourself an easy task: mediate for five minutes every day before you go to bed and build from there. Otherwise maybe go to a yoga class twice a week if that is more suitable for you. Conscious walking in a wood or park is also a good exercise to start with.

Inspiration beyond us

When you find that inspiration, which comes totally from beyond you, from something so much bigger than yourself, it feels like a flooding of the mind. You will receive meaningful and profoundly real images from that which lies at the edge of spiritual reality. You will start to see the world in a different way. You feel yourself swinging between different levels of consciousness. On one hand there is soul and spirit and on the other, mind and matter. It feels like a playground which needs to be experienced and is difficult to describe in words; characteristics change completely to what you are used to.

When you have been living your truth for a while, have been speaking up and sharing your new-found wisdom, this new paradigm comes into play. Speaking your truth has nothing to do with hurting people, or being right. It has to do with talking with your heart open, seeing other people for who they truly are, showing respect and being grateful for the life you are living. Sharing your wisdom and fulfilling your role within our humanity.

What you will see happening in your life are experiences and synchronicities which don't take you by surprise anymore. You have developed a deeper knowing, almost telling you that these occurrences are going to happen. You are experiencing flow at a deeper level, you have gone almost out of your own way.

Let me give you two examples from my own experience which happened because of conscious action. In 2012, I had been living in Holland for almost two years running the foundation, and I wanted to come back London, to be close to my children again. Something told me it would happen, I had no clue how. Sarah, my ex-wife, was moving house and asked me to come and help clear up in May, as some of my things were still in the office. There were lots of cookery books from earlier in my career and I didn't really know what to do with them. They were valuable to the right people. I wanted to give them to people who would appreciate them, so I called a food company I worked with before, and asked if they would like these books. My intuition told me that it was the right thing to do. They arranged a driver to come by. Two days later I was back in Holland and the owner rang me to thank me and invited me to lunch once I was back in London. By now it was the beginning of June, and I said I would be back on the eighteenth, my daughter's birthday. We arranged lunch for that day. I thought I would have lunch with the two owners, but something told me something magical would happen.

I arrived at the restaurant early, and they had no table booked for three people. The manager saw that there was a table for four under the same name. Immediately I knew what that meant. I sat down, and not long after the two owners arrived with their sales manager. We shared stories and I sensed that one of the owners had a burning question. Within five minutes he said, "Leon, we need you, would you like to do some work for us?"

Internally I laughed; isn't life just beautiful? I asked them what they wanted and how they saw it working as I was living in Holland. They told me the company was doing well but they also found themselves a bit stuck. As I worked with them before they knew I could help them. Immediately I made the decision to move back to London. I moved two and half weeks later, and everything just fell into place. I never looked back. The company immediately accepted my proposal for two days a week for three months, giving me the time and income to work on my foundation and other ideas which were developing. This one decision of following that deeper sense of knowing, giving the books to this company, allowed a whole domino effect to take place. Intuitively I 'knew' it was about to happen, I didn't know how, everything just fell into place.

Spiritual ego
One of the things you need to be wary about is spiritual ego. There are several kinds of ego and the most difficult to detect is spiritual ego. Within our spiritual development we may notice that we are at different points in our development than people around us. Please make no mistake about this, it is not about being better, or good versus bad. You discover that you start to see the world in a different way and that everything is connected to everything else. Spiritual ego might kick in giving us the false perception that we have arrived or that our development is complete.

I have seen many people fall prey to this; spirituality has become a new religion which can never be the meaning of true spirituality. In the next chapters we'll go into more detail. The key is to stay humble and grateful, to be aware that we are all equal and each on a different journey. When you become aware of someone who is stuck in this paradigm, be patient and understanding, send them love, and make sure you don't allow their energy too much in your own field.

For yourself, keep practising stillness, meditate and be aware of your ego where it still plays up, keep working on changing your patterns and behaviours. Look after yourself.

"The only way out is in." Leonard Jackson

The best foods

Chefs like simple dishes, done well with quality ingredients. At this stage of the process it is about the chemical breakdown of a substance by bacteria, yeasts, or other micro-organisms. In cooking that can be seen in the making of wine, beer, an air-dried ham, or sourdough bread. When you have ingredients of the best quality they are not to be messed around with: you serve them as they are, or at most with some other top quality plain ingredients.

Let's take Pata Negra ham, it comes from Spain where black-legged pigs roam freely at altitude in the mountains in the acorn season. The abundance of acorns gives a special flavour and sweetness to the meat. Pair this with the meat of these special pigs whose fat is marbled through the leg rather than on the outside, as the pigs need to work hard walking up and down the mountains.

The legs are then cured in salt and hung to dry in the air in special warehouses where the bacteria in the outside air cure the ham. They are hung for 24-36 months giving them the most amazing flavour. There is a reason this is called the best ham in the world, and is graded by specialists; something everyone should try at least once in a lifetime.

The ham can only reach the highest quality - 5J - when all the ingredients, or stages of the process are absolutely right. A good acorn season, perfect weather for the curing, top quality pigs and the finest sea salt.

Serve the ham thinly sliced on a piece of the best sourdough bread with some freshly churned organic local butter. Sourdough bread is another product where bacteria in the air produce a fresh, natural yeast, breaking down the enzymes to make the best bread, made from just the sourdough, flower, water and sea salt.

That is also what happens to us at this stage, where outside factors introduce new life into ours to strengthen us and assure the survival of our new level of being.

6 CONNECTIVE CONSCIOUSNESS

You are aware of your truth, you have found the courage to speak your truth and share it via your purpose. Now it is getting really interesting, this step is about extracting the essential meaning from your truth, to make it even purer. On an alchemical level this is distillation. Distillation is about heating a liquid until it vaporises, then cooling it until it condenses, sometimes doing that several times. This happens for example when cognac or whiskey is produced, so no impurities are left.

For the pure soul this is important, extracting the essence over heat to make sure that absolutely no impurities of the ego are left. Old or aged impurities are often very deeply submerged within ourselves. It feels like dusting the edges of your cells deep within.

You might experience small annoyances, which you thought you had dealt with are still there on a certain level. They are showing you how to become pure at every level, to distil, to understand where you are not coherent. As your heart is now fully open and you are well on track on your journey, you might experience that other people want something of you. They want to be part of that which they can see, it is intangible for them, and they feel energetically that you are making waves. Some people you encounter on your journey might not be at your level and they will overstretch themselves, as they see you as a shortcut for quick growth by tapping into your stream. Unfortunately that doesn't work. It is not a judgement, or good versus bad. We are all on our own journey and there are no shortcuts.

There might be situations on your journey where people leave you, maybe get angry at you, for no apparent reason. What happens is that they, as souls, try to fly too high, before they are really ready taking on the journey. A human being then falls back, and might blame you for what happened. This can manifest itself in a confrontation for both parties. The important thing for you is to be grateful to this person, to wish them well, you have been given a huge opportunity to learn. These are the kind of situations for your own distillation, to remove more impurities. Don't forget we can only distil something when we heat it over a fire, and so it is also for the soul.

> "All matter originates and exists only by virtue of a force which brings the particles of an atom to vibration and holds this most minute of solar systems together. We must assume behind this force the presence of a conscious intelligent mind. This mind is the matrix of all matter."
> Max Planck

Just before I returned to London in 2012, I had an experience and several signs which told me that things were changing and going to the next level. As I was running my foundation at the time, I had lived off my savings, and income was sometimes tough. In April that year I got a call from a friend who asked if I wanted to help train a chef in a tourist place in Maastricht. I said yes. The fee was way below what I would normally ask, but I was grateful for the opportunity as I needed the money.

I had a chat with the owners of the restaurant who knew nothing about my background. It was a nice popular place for tourists, the head chef was new and needed some training on staff, hygiene and procedures. It was an easy job as the cooking was very basic. The first two days I was working with the young staff and everything went fine, on the third day the head chef came back from holiday, as he was away when I arrived. After about two hours he said I could go home, that he wouldn't need me anymore. It was a beautiful day in the spring, the restaurant is situated on a very busy and beautiful square in Maastricht. I walked out into a sea of people and I was totally flabbergasted, what had just happened? This was the first time ever I was sacked, and by someone who couldn't even cook.

As I walked over the square to my home I tried not to fall into the emotion of injustice, feeling hurt or angry. I just wanted to understand what had happened. The universe gave me a big lesson. When I was running my foundation, I had always thought I could always go back to being a chef again. The truth is, once you have passed a certain point in your transformation you can't go back, you can only go forward and proceed. I now had both my feet firmly into the new paradigm, I just didn't fit anymore with the old ways, no matter how difficult this may seem.

Of course the head chef felt threatened by my knowledge and felt inferior in front of his staff. In the beginning I didn't understand why I couldn't even do this anymore. I do so much good, and what do I need to do for my income?

The lesson I received was invaluable: keep going. When you act from your heart the solution always comes. It is about trust, deep trust, as the universe will deliver, always at the very last moment. Once you are doing your inner work and following your purpose, keep going, as that is who you truly are and why you are here.

Essential meaning

"The most beautiful and deepest experience a man can have is the sense of the mysterious. It is the underlying principle of religion as well as all serious endeavour in art and science. He who can no longer pause to wonder and stand rapt in awe, is as good as dead; his eyes are closed."
Albert Einstein

As we free ourselves from all sentiments and emotions, even from our personal identity, the purification reveals your unborn self, all that you are and truly can be. The heating of the soul raises our life force repeatedly.

To just have a small understanding what the life force is, look at it this way: the universe is made up of elementary particles, but the universe can't be reduced to elementary particles. This is the most amazing thing about the universe and everything within it; we are also made up of elementary particles. When parts combine to form a whole, the whole is greater than the parts. If you take a bird apart, particle by particle, you can rebuild it exactly the same. It wouldn't be the same, however, without the life force.

Life force or consciousness may be the firing of neurons, but it can't be reduced to the activity of our mind. You might experience that ideas and thoughts just pop up in your head. However, if you look inside your brain you wouldn't find a single idea. Ideas are non-physical things, which can't be reduced to physical things.

Emotional states are related to chemicals in your body, but being in love can't be reduced to chemicals. You can't fall in love simply by reading an article on the chemicals involved. Love is something you need to experience yourself.

Now it really is getting interesting, so there is something else going on, that is the life force or consciousness. When a bird sings to mark its territory, it still doesn't explain why it sings so beautifully. The birdsong may be functional, but it's also transcendental.

It is the real mystery of life, or the mystical experience, we can't pretend it is not there. Whilst you can experience the mystical experience from your viewpoint, we can't pretend anymore that nothing else is going on. Open your eyes and look in wonder, get in tune with what is really going on around you. What is the essential meaning of our experience?

> "In your silence when there are no words, no language, nobody else is present, you are getting in tune with existence." Osho

Seeing with vision
As you are discovering more your true voice, you may also notice that a certain calmness comes over you. A trust that you are on the right path, an acceptance that you are divinely guided. You are now entering the centre of divine wisdom, where consciousness guides us.

There is truth in all things, and you are seeking this truth and meaning in everything you experience and within all aspects of yourself. Consciousness becomes your guide and experiencing everything from that place you will find yourself more in flow and understand the connection between absolutely everything.

Your vision expands and now everything you do is to support your vision, your truth and your journey to serve. That is the lesson we can learn from great people like Nelson Mandela, Mother Teresa and Mahatma Ghandi. Just like us they were on a journey, a journey of discovery and trust. They had access to the same life force and consciousness we have now.

The difference between most of us and great leaders like these is that they had a 100% belief and trust in their vision, and were absolutely convinced they would make it happen. Ghandi had a vision so big, for the British to leave India that nobody would take him seriously. Almost on his own he started working on it. The seemingly impossible was achieved only a few decades later.

We all know about the trials and tribulations, and ultimately the transformation Mandela went through during his life and captivity. For me, most of his success and the inspiration he became to millions was due to that transformation, and the balanced and serene personality he developed. It was their clear vision and belief which helped them achieve their amazing feats for humanity. If you look at such leaders you can see that they were working on something that was no longer about them anymore. Each and every one of us can achieve something like that. Another important point is that for these legends, it wasn't about them, it was about something a lot bigger then themselves, and they were truly in service to all of us.

Now compare them to some of the leaders and politicians we have nowadays. Truly understanding who you are and living your purpose, is not about you, it is not about being famous or having your name on the cover of a magazine or in the papers. That might come as a result, but it is never the aim. Think of the life of a single flower, referred to earlier... Just follow your inner vision.

> "Be soft in your practice. Think of the method as a fine silvery stream, not a raging waterfall. Follow the stream, have faith in its course. It will go its own way, meandering here, trickling there. It will find the grooves, the cracks, the crevices. Just follow it. Never let it out of your sight. It will take you." Sheng-Yen

In the summer of 2012, I was settling in again in London, close to the children, doing my consultancy job and supporting my foundation from a distance. My life was a rollercoaster and many events told me it was time to move on, to bring my truth again to a higher level. As happens in these cases, you get the signs, you hear people saying just the right things. What I got every time was, "Leon, share your message, people need to hear it, and you are an inspiration".

I knew my purpose: No-one to bed hungry, and that is not just about food. I understood bringing it to a higher level was to awaken the fire within others for them to find their own purpose, to life on a higher vibration. I discovered through the turmoil which happened that summer that my gift is that I see people for who they truly are. My gift is that people feel trusted around me, they open their heart and I can reflect back to them what I see at their core, I can see who they truly are.

These were powerful insights, I was here to do a lot more then my foundation. My whole journey, everything over the years prepared me to fulfil my role. There was no turning back now. I was inspiring others. The constant purification of your soul ensures that you constantly go to a higher, purer level. Now I was on a new quest. How could I bring forth my deepest truth, how could I inspire others in the best way? What I found was amazing. Just be you, and the purer you will become. You live that way just by showing up as yourself. People understand, they can feel it energetically, there is immediately a trust, and as you show up fully as yourself you are already inspiring and encouraging others to do the same. Just as Mandela, Ghandi and Mother Teresa and many others did.

Different dimensions

Scientifically it is proven that time and space don't really exist and time is not linear to the way we experience it as human beings. We experience time on earth because of the speed we travel through the universe and the gravity we experience. As you become lighter metaphysically you will experience time in a whole different way. When you are lighter you 'travel' through your journey a lot faster as there is less to hold you back, less resistance, in other words less gravity.

Just think of going to the grocery store and carrying two heavy bags on the way home; they slow you down. Emotions and patterns work exactly the same way. We live in a three-dimensional world and it is often said that there are different dimensions in which our spirit lives. In these different dimensions you see the world in a different way, from a different perspective, and we can have access to these dimensions.

Let me try to explain in a simple way how that works and what it would change for you to experience, let's say, the third dimension. As humans we live in the third dimension which means we can only see the world in two dimensions. Imagine you are looking for your car again on this big outside parking lot, you can't find it as you can only see the cars in front and to the side of you. You can't see beyond them. Now someone is again in the apartment block on the 6th floor and they say to you, "Your car is two rows on your left", as they have a different vision. We live in the third dimension, yet we can only see two dimensions. Seeing in three dimensions would mean that we could look into buildings and cars, different to having X-ray vision.

Metaphysically this is exactly the same, sometimes when you talk to someone, you might get an insight, some knowledge you receive about that person you couldn't possibly know. This means you get that insight from a higher dimension. As you are growing, and becoming lighter on your journey, you are experiencing these moments more often. You are in tune. Accessing the fourth dimension does mean you have a different perspective and you can see what is really going on for yourself or others.

These insights you receive now are there to help you grow and to assist others in their journey, and for you to be of service to them. In the beginning you will be experience these occurrences occasionally; as you get more experienced they will become a regular feature and you actually learn to access the fourth dimension as you wish. The knowledge you get here is what truly connects you with your core and with your collective consciousness. In the fifth dimension time doesn't exist and everything happens in an instant. You might experience it at times, where you intuitively feel there is something you need and it shows up instantly, as a miracle. This means you have briefly experienced the fifth dimension. On your journey now you will be experiencing these moments more often, you will waver backwards and forwards in between the different stages.

Savour those moments, be aware and grateful when they happen, and keep working on yourself and you will experience an immense growth rate, being more and more in the higher dimensions. You will experience life in a totally different way, everything will feel easier to deal with and you will be able to distinguish and let go of many of your third dimensional emotions, as they don't exist in that reality.

"We have come into this exquisite world to experience ever more deeply our divine courage, freedom and light!"
Hafiz

About light

Much has been written about being the light and seeing the light. Light is the basic energy of the universe. Light is what you and I are made of. I don't want to repeat many of the great quotes and what is already written about it. It is important for you to always remember your light; that is who you truly are, and to turn your light on as other people can see and recognise it.

Remind yourself on a daily basis that you are a wonderful being, as this is the first step in your ongoing transformational journey. One of my mentors always said to me. "Don't try to see the light, be the light." Too many of us put others on a pedestal and look up to them, having them as an example of a shining light. The challenge with this is that you always need another light in order to keep yourself lit. When you are the light, you don't need anyone else to do that for you, you shine your light on others. Remember when you try to see the light, you get blinded. Look into the sun for a while when it is at its highest point, it is impossible to keep looking at it, its light is so sharp.

The sun gives its light to us always, it just shines. On the inside there are lots of processes and combustion going on for the sun to shine. It gives its light to us all, it will never say you don't deserve its light. At this stage of our journey you have become light and this is the way to live your life now. You make an impact to everyone who comes in your path, they can see your light, share it with them. This can be by just a smile or a friendly word, the impact you are making will increase immediately. On a universal level there is no difference between the small or large actions we undertake, that is only what we think as human beings. Each action, big or small, is as important metaphysically. Think about nature where a small flower is as important as a huge mahogany tree in the Amazon rainforest.

> "The stillness in stillness is not the real stillness; only when there is stillness in movement does the universal rhythm manifest."
> Bruce Lee

There is something magical about not knowing; we believe there is so much we still need to know and learn. As you must have experienced in the past, the courses you took led you away from who you truly are, just because you felt you had to learn something. What happens then is that it takes you away from your light. Imagine that you already know everything you need to know, you have access to your collective consciousness and all you do is to just keep shining your light, your brilliance.

Isaac Newton, Leonardo Da Vinci and Albert Einstein were true alchemists who knew they had to understand the spiritual laws behind anything in order to change something in their current reality. It is not common knowledge, but Newton spent most of his time on alchemy and understanding the deeper reality behind everything.

In 1666 when Newton was at Cambridge University it was actually closed for two years because of the plague. In those two years he couldn't research and learn as he would normally do. In these two years Newton came up with most of his laws like the universal law of gravity. During this two-year period he let go of the conventional way of learning and by tapping into something bigger than him he had his most creative period. It started when he tried to calculate the motion of the moon around earth. This was really the start of modern science.

We see many child prodigies doing something very similar. In a conventional way they don't really fit in to what we believe is the norm in our present culture. Some get labelled autistic, for example, as our education and medical system love to put them in a box. Many of these children are brilliant in just one aspect, and at a very young age come up with ideas or inventions which just leaves us stunned. A three-year-old might play the piano like a real virtuoso, and recently an eleven-year-old invented solar panels which are 70% more effective than the ones we use, just by looking at nature. A fourteen-year-old child invented a method to clean our oceans within three years. There are many more examples, the interesting fact for me is that these children just shine their light, they connect to our collective consciousness.

As souls they are so developed they understand what their role is and they just shine. Nothing more, nothing less. What if we all do that? I'm interested to see what the world would look like then, aren't you?

"Darkness cannot drive out darkness; only light can do that. Hate cannot drive out hate; only love can do that."
Martin Luther King, Jr.

As Martin Luther King said, only light can drive out darkness. This goes for all the challenges in your life. When you come across something which might challenge you or a difficult situation, we can only solve that by shining light or love upon the problem, nothing else. When you discover a challenge for yourself or a pattern you are stuck in, shine your light. Look at what holds you back and shine your light, with positive energy and love. Switch on the light just as you would do in your living room. When there is light there simply can't be darkness.

Light needs to be circulated, it never gets lost. When sunlight hits something on earth, it gets reflected and can then work its magic on something else, or the light gets absorbed and turns into energy. I can only see reasons for you to shine your light, and your light comes directly from source, from consciousness.

When you are at this stage of your transformational journey you will experience a moment when you must let go of your core or default setting. This is the pattern you took on in this three-dimensional reality in which you live; it is your survival mode. It has protected you to survive in the dream and culture in which you have grown up. Now it is time to let go of this pattern. Although it might have served you well, it is now holding you back becoming who you truly are, on every level.

Just at the point when you think you have done a lot of work, and things are going swimmingly, letting go might be a tough experience. When there is more light, there is also more darkness. In order to shine more you need to go to your darkest place. Once you are ready, spirit will give you the opportunity to let go of your default setting. This can be tough; be aware it is the most liberating experience you will encounter and is necessary in order for you to go to the next level.

My default setting for most of my life was to be number one. I have described to you how I was looking to be number one in everything I did. I stopped doing something, or wasn't even interested anymore if I thought I couldn't excel. In April 2011, when I was still living in Holland, two people - one who knew me and another who didn't - both said to me, "Leon, you are trying to prove yourself again." My answer was easy: "Who, me? Of course not, I let go of that ages ago."

Their comments kept going round in my mind and they were right, however. Deep inside there was still that young boy who wanted to prove he was good enough. Luckily the universe was working with me and thought it was time for me to let go of this limited belief and heal my hurt. A week later, on a beautiful spring day of about 27 degrees, I was lying in bed, all wrapped up but feeling very cold. I was shivering and shaking, I knew it wasn't an illness; intuitively I knew that I was letting go of that belief of mine on a deep level. I felt lonely, was in pain, and was literally shaking for two days.

When a thought keeps going around it becomes a belief, and those beliefs come from a higher vibration to our present reality into a lower vibration and they will settle in our bodies. That can make us ill in different forms. My patterns, and striving to be number one as my default setting, was something so deep; it wasn't enough to just leave my thoughts. It also had to disappear on a physical level, and that is what happened that weekend. It was tough; I felt very bad, but I knew it had to happen and I experienced it as something very liberating.

"It's not the daily increase but daily decrease. Hack away at the unessential."
Bruce Lee

The saucier
The saucier is the alchemist of the kitchen, especially in a traditional kitchen, where the magic takes place making sauces. We saw earlier from simple ingredients like egg and butter a light fluffy and rich sauce is produced by changing the reality. A saucier is the person who is responsible for all the sauces and the cooking of the meat dishes. It is usually the section in a kitchen given to the most experienced chef.

A sauce is often the component in a dish which brings everything together and is the key ingredient between an ordinary dish and a special one. Most sauces are produced by carefully reducing a liquid, to keep the pure essence of that ingredient, sometimes adding a stock which is carefully extracted from fine ingredients, and then one by one adding additional ingredients at different stages.

It was definitely my favourite section of the kitchen and it was my speciality. Nothing was more rewarding than standing over a saucepan and carefully crafting the recipe and flavour. Speciality dishes and sauces get better over time once you've practised and rehearsed making them hundreds of times. A bit like your own transformational journey, every time you come across a challenge, a pattern or something which disturbs you, with the right attitude you can turn these around into gifts and opportunities to learn in an instant.

The recipe I have given you here is a personal favourite of mine. Braised beef in red wine sauce, a stew where you cook the meat and make the sauce at the same time. A typical dish you can perfect over time and which can only be done well when you take your time. No shortcuts!

Daube de boeuf
Serves 4
- 2.75 kg ox cheeks
- 1 onion
- 1 carrot
- 1 leek
- 1 head of garlic, cloves peeled
- 1 sprig of thyme
- 1 bay leaf
- 1.5 bottle of good red wine
- enough veal stock to cover
- fresh pepper and salt

Remove all the fat from the ox cheeks and cut each in 4 pieces.

Peel all the vegetables and cut into large pieces. Put the vegetables and meat in a bowl and add the wine, garlic and herbs. Cover with cling film and put in the fridge for 4-24 hours.

When you are ready, take the meat out of the wine, dry with some kitchen paper, add pepper and salt and fry the meat in the olive oil until golden brown. Transfer the meat to a pan large enough to hold all the ingredients. Repeat until all the meat is done, then brown the vegetables. Reduce the wine in a separate pan until reduced by half. Add the wine and vegetables to the meat.

Preheat the oven to 180 degrees Celsius.

Add the veal stock so everything is covered, bring to a slow simmer and cover with a lid or tin foil.

Put the dish in the oven and cook slowly for 3.5 - 4 hrs. Carefully take the meat out of the sauce and keep warm. Reduce the sauce and sieve, flavour the sauce if necessary with some pepper and salt, a touch of vinegar and maybe a knob of butter.

Serve with light creamy mash potatoes, fried wild mushrooms and baby onions.

Force versus power

> "The Master doesn't try to be powerful, thus he is truly powerful. The ordinary man keeps reaching for power; thus he never has enough."
> Lao Tzu

There is a lot of confusion and misunderstanding about power and force. Power is unfortunately a word which, in our culture, is misused and misunderstood. Some people love to have power while others shy away from it. What in our modern lives we perceive as power is actually force. People in power force things upon others and that is not how nature intended. That can be the laws government put upon us, by a leader or group of people who believe they have certain rights above others. It can be a company which enforces certain regulations which are beyond reasonable measure just because they believe they have the power. Also many parents who don't know well how to deal with their children enforce certain rules on the children without seeing them as equals. That is force; force comes from misconceived power which, to me, is fear.

What is true power? Power is something beautiful, and which exists also in nature for the common good. Let's look at our earth. Earth is definitely in its natural power. Because earth sits in its true authentic power it attracts everything it needs. Through its authentic power a field is created which we call gravity, and because of gravity, which is a power, earth attracts everything it needs in order to fulfil its purpose. It is as simple as that.

Now imagine when you look at yourself, the more you live from your true core, the more you experience living in your authentic power, and the right people and opportunities will gravitate towards you. The more this happens the more abundance you will experience. The same goes for a mighty oak tree or the mahogany tree in the Amazon rainforest, they are in their true power and attract what they need.

True power is magical and something we should aim for. Stay away from force, as force comes from fear. I also come across people who shy away from their authentic power and say, for example that they don't want to be a leader. A leader is someone we associate as something from the current paradigm, someone who acts with force. I believe a true leader is someone who acts from within their true core, and uses their authentic power to fulfil their purpose for the greater good. In that sense we can all be a leader and we shouldn't shy away from our role.

You are now on the point of your journey that you have merged with collective consciousness, the ego no longer controls you, you are a balanced human being, and as a leader it is your role to bring out your creative self. As you now have entered the higher forces, you are able to manifest all your unique leadership qualities in a balanced and serene way.

"Those who flow as life flows know they need no other force."
Lao Tzu

7 YOUR AUTHENTIC POWER

You have now arrived at the final step of your journey, even though the transformational journey is an ongoing one. When you achieve this step you'll have mastered all the levels. You have found a new confidence which is beyond all things, which comes from a permanent state of consciousness which embodies your highest aspirations, that of the world around you and the collective good.

> "Thus you will have the glory of the whole world. All obscurity will be clear to you. This is the strong power of all powers because it overcomes everything fine and penetrates everything solid."
> The Emerald Tablets

The Emerald tablets were found in ancient Egypt and are said to be the basis of all knowledge and alchemy. In alchemy this final step is called coagulation, to change a substance from liquid back to a solid or semi-solid state. This can be, for example, curdled cheese; it is the sublimation of the purified element. The perfect element!

When you have perfected this step you will have found peace and can be at peace in every situation you encounter. No mean feat, but there is still some work to be done.

You will have become pure light again and that is who we truly are. This re-emerging of our real selves brings together the purest essence of our soul, body and matter. It will reflect in our life experiences, and will feel like a new found personality which enables you to deal with and go through all that life gives you. You experience a new-found balance in your life.

You are directly connected to your pure essence, to the life force; this state fills you with love, light and grace as it comes from something which is far bigger than yourself. You live in the present moment and in harmony with everything around you. What is this new-found wisdom in action? How do you achieve this new balance and perspective and for your soul to be serene and generous?

> "Less and less do you need to force things, until finally you arrive at non-action. When nothing is done, nothing is left undone."
> Lao Tzu

Lao Tzu was the author of the Tao Te Ching, in which he talked about The Way or the Art of Living. It is the oldest book known about this knowledge and is said to be the basis of Buddhism. How do we achieve this state where we are totally in flow with the energies around us?

For example, a good athlete can enter a state of total awareness in which she hits the right stroke or movement seemingly by itself, without any effort. Not consciously, it is the purest form of being; she is totally one with her surroundings.

This comes after years of training and achieving mastery, yet at the pivotal moment totally trusting instincts and the natural energies. Many athletes or artists have spoken about the moments when they are so in flow with what they are doing that nothing else seems to exist bar being one with the experience. This really is the state of consciousness we are describing here.

The athlete or artist has totally and wholeheartedly vanished into the act. This void or vacuum which seems to occur is actually the place where everything happens. There is a trust for the higher intelligence of the body or consciousness to guide the performance. It is acting with the softness of water and is guided by the energies which are naturally around you.

Living in harmony

Imagine living in total harmony with the way things are and giving up all concepts, judgements and desires, where your mind has grown naturally compassionate and one with everything around you. This means that you truly have mastered nature; the way things really are! It is not about conquering the natural way but becoming it. You will have found deep within yourself the central truth and the essence of the art of living.

The more solitary we are, the more compassionate we can be; the more we let go of what we love, the more present our love becomes; the clearer our insight into what is beyond good and evil, the more we can embody the good. Until finally you are able to say, in all humility, "I am in harmony."

"He who knows other men is discerning; he who knows himself is intelligent. He who overcomes others is strong; he who overcomes himself is mighty." Lao Tzu

Once we arrive at this level, we will face challenges from a totally different perspective, from the balance and peace which we have established within ourselves. When there is more light, so also more darkness will be present. The challenges might become even bigger, in order to test you and keep you at the highest level of your true being. The beauty is that you can deal with the challenges in a lighter way and see them for what they are, looking from the distance.

Generally we never like it when these deep challenges show up. We must be grateful, however, as they are opportunities for us to grow and let go in order to become more pure and empty.

At the beginning of 2014, I had a deep challenge myself. A year before a woman came into our lives who claimed she had done many good things in the world. However nothing was traceable, she had an explanation for everything. Not long after we met she was invited onto the board of my foundation and slowly we started doing some work together with an international group, doing good in the world.

Intuitively I felt that a few things weren't right. I didn't immediately listen to my intuitions well enough, as she came highly recommended and I believed everyone should be given a chance.

At the end of 2013, I couldn't deny my intuition anymore. Too many stories just weren't adding up any more. It was a difficult situation as some family and people I work with were involved. By this time she was part of the board of my foundation and I discovered that she was making up all of her stories! I must admit she was very good at it; after all she had been practising all her life.

Then at the start of 2014, I realised that since she had come on board no real progress had been made. Many initiatives had come to a halt, I uncovered some of the lies she had been telling and my eyes truly opened up. I decided to give her the benefit of the doubt. One day when she and I were sitting in her garden, just the two of us, I confronted her with a few of my concerns. Her reaction was amazing. She turned on me immediately, started accusing me of many different things; that I lied, that I wasn't honest or sincere. It really was an avalanche of accusations.

I left was flabbergasted and I left her house. The few weeks afterwards were very difficult. She was of course afraid to be found out, and what I realised was that her whole life was built on lies and deceit, and not just with us and the work we were doing. Everything around her, with her husband, her friends and some other initiatives she was involved with. For her the risk to be uncovered was so high that she started hitting back at those around her in order to save herself.

I had to cut the ties, that took time and a lot of pain, as family and friends were involved. She kept firing on all cylinders, spreading lies and bad stories and that made it very difficult. The lesson for me was that, even though I didn't manage all of the time, the more I stayed balanced and grounded and watched the situation from a higher perspective - my new-found personality - I could see what was really going on and let myself be guided by the energy. I had great people around me supporting me and I am now grateful for the experience. This short story might not fully describe the intensity of what happened without going into too much detail, but I have grown so much because of it and come closer to my core.

It confirmed to me that I have journeyed a long way and that I am on the right path, becoming lighter, more peaceful and more in harmony all the time. Look at these experiences in your own life from this perspective and see them as gifts to stay balanced and at peace. In nature all will go back to its roots.

I learned who I truly am, to live again from my highest vibration, and to trust myself more, let myself be guided by my intuition even when the outside world tries to tell me differently.

> "Embracing the Way, you become embraced.
> Breathing gently, you become new-born.
> Clearing your mind, you become clear.
> Nurturing your children, you become impartial.
> Opening your heart, you become accepted.
> Accepting the world, you embrace the Way."
> Peter Mendel

Understanding nature

Some of you might ask what it means to understand nature and to fully live accordingly. Look at it this way: do the heavens revolve? Does the earth stand still? Do the sun and the moon contend for their positions? The sun and the moon are just there fulfilling their role, and one is not jealous of the other or want that position. Life or nature isn't about that. The sun and the moon just continue to revolve inevitably on their own accord in sync with everything around them.

We often ask ourselves which came first: the chicken or the egg? Let me ask you another question: Do clouds make rain or does the rain make clouds? There is no real answer to it, both follow the energies which are there, what I called life force. This is the same energy which lets the sun come up and shine for millions of years and the tides of the oceans rise. It is there but we can't see it, we can't hear it, but we can be in tune with it and let ourselves be guided effortlessly. That is to be one with nature.

When you are in harmony with nature, which encompasses absolutely everything, you only need to walk it. To allow the energy to go through you means being empty enough on the inside for the energy to pass through you and do its work. You have to let go of all that still stops you.

In 2008, I was lucky enough and grateful to be one of the handful of foreigners in New Delhi to be present at the 60th commiseration of Ghandi's death. It was a beautiful day of ceremonies with representatives from all over India. At the end we spoke to the last living student of Ghandi and we asked her, "If there is one thing you would like to share with us about Ghandi, what would that be?" She told us that one day they were walking on the beach and someone asked Ghandi what he strived for. Ghandi stopped walking and drew a large circle with his stick in the sand. There was a silence, and he explained, "To be zero". To be zero means to be totally open for the forces to work through you, the beginning is in the end. It took me quite some time to understand what Ghandi meant. It is, however, the most wonderful thing, to be totally in flow as nature intended. Be zero!

Let me explain what I mean by the beginning is in the end. You really have to go to the end, when there is nothing left to let go of, only then will everything we have been talking about at the highest level start to happen.

Ghandi truly understood what it meant to live in flow, reacting to the energies and flowing with them just like water, and he achieved what he set out to do. The British occupation stopped not long after his death, as a result of him relentlessly working on his path, the big bold vision, taking small steps all the time. The energy which he transmuted, most of the time unseen, allowed for others to start supporting him and his cause. A large river might not be able to move a giant rock, yet by gently flowing, the river can wear the rock down slowly with its gentle forces - erosion.

Think about the child prodigies I mentioned earlier who work with the energies within to achieve the most amazing and unbelievable results, even if the whole world can't make sense of them. It is not that any one of these children are special, they are in a place where they listen and flow with what is presented to them, even if we can't make any rational sense of it. They are in touch with consciousness.

Wu Wei or nothingness

The concept of Wu Wei comes from the Tao. It describes what Ghandi refers to as zero. It means not doing and leaving space for the energy to flow through. Trusting the process of the universe as you are part of it rather than controlling it. You empty yourself of everything and maintain a steady serenity. Knowing that all things take shape in the right order and time. When you look at nature that all happens in a divine order. Understanding that all things take shape and become before returning to their source. Like a flower which grows and flourishes and then returns to its roots. Returning to source is the true serenity and destiny.

When you are totally at peace with yourself you can be really reflective of what you see happening around you, rather than being proactive and striving to achieve. You can compare it to being like water. Water always finds its own level and it flows with the force which is moving it. It flows through every hole, it takes the shape of whatever container it is in, it flows around every obstacle yet is achieves everything it needs to depending on the force which is used.

Imagine we, as human beings, can be in a state like that!

When you achieve this state you will find that you have become an instrument of the eternal way. You are sensitive to everything which happens around you, and on each level, you have stopped to control and are fully aware of your own constraints, requirements and outcomes.

Earlier I spoke about your default setting. Before truly mastering this level it is important that you take care of your deepest fear. This is another difficult one as you first need to know your highest purpose. My purpose is: no-one to bed hungry; I discovered that a few years ago and it made total sense to me. Everything I have been doing since has to do with fulfilling my purpose, and as life goes sometimes things didn't always go to plan. A few months ago I was walking with a friend in a park in London, just before I started writing my book and I told her this story about an accountant I know.

I had just received an email from her where she promoted an Australian guy who helps you to discover your greatest fear by letting you say your purpose a number of times quickly, and then he plays it backwards. When I discussed this a while ago with another friend he said to me, that's easy, I can do that myself, and it works". He told me what he learned. I wanted to do it myself but forgot about it.

That day in the park I asked my friend for a pen and paper and started to write my purpose backwards. It took me some time, some puzzling, saying it out loud, but then I had it: Why are we good but not enough? I looked at it several times, to be sure I made no mistake. It was unbelievable!

Why are we good but not enough? That is exactly how I always felt, whenever I was with my peers as a top chef, going to a conference where I needed to speak, or even on a date. I always knew I was good but something told me I was not good enough. I believed it fully as I thought there was still so much I needed to do.

I was amazed, first of all I saved myself a few thousand dollars, and most importantly I could work on it. I know I am a special human being with great qualities which I have to share with the world, and inspire others. Time to let go of one of the last remaining pieces. Try this exercise for yourself and see what your deepest fear is.

The concept of Wu Wei is difficult to understand and against all principles we believe in our current culture. It is about being carefree, seemingly aimlessly wandering through life. Being in the right place at the right time. Have you ever experienced that you can be in this place all the time, where the right things just happen? There are three principles to it:
- effortlessness
- responsiveness
- unobtrusiveness

To obtain this truth within yourself you need to be free of all limitations, as these are what holds you back from achieving this miracle state.

Free of limitations
Imagine that you are free of all limitations. The nothingness I described earlier is not passiveness, it is simply accepting what inevitably goes around. When you are free of all the limitations of your mind you feel no need any more to force things to happen. You see everything in a fresh light and not

time-related anymore.

To be free of all limitations is to be free of everything your mind and ego believe you need to do or own. It is what Ghandi strived for, it is what nature lives for. Look at animals; they just live their life, still fulfilling their purpose. Butterflies are often used as a metaphor for transformation; they just fly seemingly aimlessly around in the garden. We can't stop looking at butterflies, and with that a butterfly does everything it needs to do. Could we as human beings not just use the transformation from the cocoon to the butterfly as a metaphor? Could we also use the way it lives as a metaphor for our own lives? Why not, I say.

We constantly need to look at ourselves in every situation: how am I feeling, how am I reacting, am I balanced, what is coming up for me? By this constant polishing of our mirror we can stay balanced and at peace. Each time an issue comes up, following the movement of the energies, practising rituals and ceremonies can be very important. Make sure that you have set times in your day where you find the stillness within. Connect regularly and keep in touch with people around you often who have arrived at this beautiful balanced place of peace within.

A daily practice of meditation is important to connect with your higher self. It helps you to stay balanced during the day and react to whatever happens from that peace. Just as an athlete trains his muscles, it is important for us to stay in touch with the harmony within and to train our 'muscles'. Each day we wear clean clothes to start the day fresh; practicing meditation and getting in tune is exactly the same.

Find other rituals which work for you. This could be yoga, or walking in nature on a regular basis. I can't stress the importance of this enough.

> "The first and foremost thing that you owe to yourself is to be 100% straight, at least with yourself"
> Sadhguru

You are now at your core, the purified element: who you truly are. This will rejuvenate you into a perfect vessel of health for your body and soul. Your new-found being and energy will nourish and energise you on every level, it will help you to effortlessly achieve everything you set out to do. Remember that you now have permanent access to this state of higher consciousness which embodies your highest aspirations.

You'll need to embody all parts of yourself, it is the sacred union of your lower and higher self. Nature requires a balance between polarities to exist, think yin and yang and remember that these polarities will always show up in nature and in your life. Day and night, hot and cold, right or wrong. Live with the natural laws as simply as possible and trust the process of the universe, as you are part of it rather than controlling it.

The question "What does it mean to be human in Sufism?" is usually answered with: the universal man. The idea of the universal man, sometimes called the perfect man, is really independent of any philosophical descriptions of it, in fact those are also found in Greek and Neoplatonic sources. According to these sources the perfect or universal man is the reality containing all the levels of existence. It includes all the latent possibilities in each of those levels, a reality that, in those who have acknowledged it within themselves, male or female, has become fully realised.

What this means is that person who has realised it is the prototype of the human state, both male and female, and the prototype of the cosmos. It is what in other convictions is often described as the cross. To connect the higher and lower realms with each other, that is the vertical part. To be fully connected with consciousness and grounded in this physical reality. To be fully human is represented with the horizontal bar of the cross. It means to be fully balanced and at peace with oneself and the universe. The two parts of a cross meet in the centre, where our heart is. Jesus returned to heaven when he died on the cross, a metaphor for what we as humans try to achieve. To become the perfect man.

Jesus had his arms spread fully open showing that even at the time when he was killed he had his heart fully open. That is the real message from that story, later through the doctrine which we call religion the message got totally changed and misinterpreted, unfortunately. There is so much beauty and truth in these metaphors.

Wider issues
As human beings we have the tendency to interfere with the natural occurrence of events; we actually believe that is our natural state. However earlier we have seen that our natural state is just to be and allow, to flow. Non-action is the right response to life; this, however doesn't mean doing nothing, but it means reacting to energies in the right way with the right amount of focus and action.

Look for example at the Dalai Lama; he embodies this state we call Wu Wei. He is totally at peace with himself and he radiates that energy beautifully, in such a way that he has millions of people adoring him, he is their inspiration. He didn't achieve it by shouting from the rooftops or having a marketing and PR company advising him on every move. The Dalai Lama reacted to whatever occurred in his life in the right way, he connected to the wisdom of the universe and shared freely with the world around him. Do you understand what he achieved by being still?

Non-action, how strange it might feel, is the right response. Allowing and trusting the universe that the right opportunities will show up. The communion with nature is key to this, as the more you allow this to happen and understand it, you will start to live a simple life. That life might look simple on the outside, however it gives you all the beauty, love and light on the inside. In this context, the simple life means that you are not attached, searching or wanting for material possessions anymore in order to achieve happiness, peace and balance within your life. I can't repeat it often enough: the outside world is a reflection of the inside world and never the other way around.

When you arrive at that stage where the mystical union happens between all that is you, you can only realise that you are here to fulfil what we can now call your divine role. The role each and every one has within our humanity on this planet and as part of consciousness is as important, just like every cell of our body is as important and just fulfils its role.

It doesn't matter how big what you do in our material world is, a young woman who decides to look after her grandmother is as important as the director of a large charity or someone who travels the world inspiring others. What does matter is that you listen and act from the balance and peace within and follow what you are guided to, and to do that task with the right intention. Be a compassionate leader and fulfil your task with humility and reserve.

The wider issues of the world will become important to you; you will not only just realise this, you will start to live this from every part of your being. It will give you the most pleasure and gratitude, it also ensures that you stay balanced and at peace as fulfilling your role is the thing which comes so naturally to you. It gives you energy rather than costing energy.

Bees fly around all day pollinating the flowers and as a result collect honey. They do this effortlessly as it is their natural state. We can look at many other examples in nature where sometimes whole herds of animals move all at the same time to a new place, as intuitively they know where they need to be or what they need to do. There is no doubt or fear or even a voice which tells them: surely it can't be like this.

You now live in a place where you will have absolute faith and trust to what is. Being so connected and in tune with nature, it is your duty to look after what brought you here. Just a flower or tree has a duty to take care of the ecosystem around it. We have that same duty, to acknowledge where we came from, to rise and give back to it nature.

> "Our task is to unite humanity throughout the world. However, if you act as an individual, you will never be able to achieve that."
> Nelson Mandela

Understanding your purpose and gift and sharing both without holding back is the challenge, when we have a world around us which might not have developed as far as we have. Stay balanced and grounded and keep listening to your inner core and connect regularly, often and deeply with those around you who you can share your journey with.

Being guided by higher forces

Oneness is a concept which you will have heard about and which becomes easier to understand and accept as your progress on your transformational journey continues. We are all one, and we are all unique. I have used the example of a flock of birds before and that is for me exactly how it works. We are all made up from the same atoms and particles which are flying around in the universe and were here in the beginning all those billions of years ago.

Look at our oneness and recognise that every person is a mirror or reflection of yourself, accept that each of us is on their own journey with their own challenges and instructions, which are not always obvious. When you look at people from the perspective that they are just like you and me, we are one. Your world will again change to a new perspective and new heights. You will deepen your own inner peace and understanding of who you truly are and why you are here.

Understanding our oneness will give you a certain humility and acceptance of your role within the greater good. You will understand that what you do on every level or what others do, even if this is on the other side of the world, affects all of us immediately and on the same scale. We don't experience problems anymore as ours or theirs. Our oneness teaches us that everything which happens on our planet is for our collective interest. Good or bad, remember that next time when you see something happening in the world or when you throw things away that you don't need anymore.

As you are now in the final step of the journey and your intuition is very strong, you 'know' what is going on at many levels. You have strengthened your understanding of consciousness. It is fairly simple, we are souls having a human experience and some parts of our soul or spirit are still in a different dimension at this moment.

As you have exercised your senses, and have become more aware, you may notice that you receive more messages coming to you from spirit, from other souls. You might feel guided all of a sudden what to do or say, yet you can't explain where that information is coming from.

As you have emptied yourself of all restraints, you are now open to receive from different realms; they will make themselves known to you when you are ready for them. This is nothing weird or strange, it simply means that you are now ready to receive information which will help you even further on your journey whilst staying balanced and at peace. Explore these feelings, insights or signs, appreciate them, even talk to the voices you hear and thank them. Be grateful.

Over time these experiences will multiply and become stronger, you can even ask them for guidance in any situation. That is truly living in the moment and being at peace.

"I feel that the essence of spiritual practice is your attitude toward others. When you have a pure, sincere motivation, then you have the right attitude toward others based on kindness, compassion, love and respect. Practice brings the clear realisation of the oneness of all human beings and the importance of others benefiting by your actions."
The Dalai Lama

Pure ingredients
As we are talking about the highest state here and an ingredient has become perfected, there is nothing a chef should with do it, to change it or add to it. Just to serve it on its own.

At the beginning of the chapter I mentioned curdled cheese, which after ripening can become a great cheese, like an old Parmesan, Roquefort or a beautiful raw milk Brie. Even in the best restaurants, cheese is honoured and served on its own maybe with a handful of condiments.

In the winter season you sometimes see these two perfect ingredients combined; a ripe farmhouse Brie laced with lashing of winter truffles - they complement each other wonderfully.

Take a Brie which needs about another week or so of ripening, cut it open horizontally and open the two sides up. Slice a large black winter truffle in very thin slices and lay the slices on top of one side of the Brie, and add a few drops of olive oil. Lay the other side of the Brie back on top of the truffles as if the cheese is assembled again, wrap in cling film and refrigerate for a week.

Take the cheese out of the fridge about an hour before serving and serve slices of the cheese with a simple green salad and a very light dressing.

Enjoy!

8 ALCHEMY MADE EASY

Your transformational journey is the most beautiful journey you can undertake, it is the biggest gift you can give to yourself, and at times it might feel lonely or testing and will make absolutely no sense. You might feel you are working hard on yourself, and challenge after challenge is thrown at you. You might understand why these occur on your path, at times it just seems there is no end to them.

We all experience these feelings at times and in order to stay focused and see the bigger picture I have compiled a list of helpful tips, suggestions and general things you can do and think about to help you stay on your journey, balanced and peaceful. Wherever you are, at the beginning or more advanced, all these pointers and suggestions have helped me and others enormously.

Have a look through them and revisit them regularly, see which ones fit for you, and where you can improve. They are in no particular order; look around and the right courses, books, meetings or people will present themselves to you. The most important thing is that knowledge and wisdom are not learned from books but from living life, it is an experiential process.

You already have everything you need to live your life as who you truly are. You have all the resources, connections, ideas and wisdom within you. As children we inherently know why we are here, we are still more pure as beings. When we get older we become more influenced by the people around us and the experiences we have in the culture in which we live. There will be a moment in your life when your purpose becomes clear to you. The challenge always is: do you dare, do you have enough courage and understanding to fulfil your purpose, to be fully you?

When I was seven years old, in 1973, there was a famine in Africa. We were one of the first people in our street with one of those huge full colour TVs. In those days, Africa really was the other side of the planet and you would never think that one day you would visit it. There were images on TV all the time of dying children and animals; luckily we don't portray these disasters in this way anymore.

One evening I didn't want to eat my vegetables - overcooked broad beans in a white sauce - as I didn't like them. My mother said, "Eat your vegetables, there are children starving in Africa who would love your beans." I remember thinking how would my two tablespoons of beans help those children? One day I will do something about it, but now I don't want to eat these beans.

I can still vividly see the image of this happening all those years ago, just as clear as I can see the room I am sitting in now. I became aware again of this particular dinner in our house when I was reading The Alchemist by Paolo Coelho a few years ago. He writes: "We all know our purpose as children, and one day later in life it will come back to you, it is then up to you what you do about it." Not long after this realisation I started my foundation and my life changed.

Food became the real thread during my life and my foundation has helped thousands of children. My purpose, no-one to bed hungry, has evolved to a higher level and I am blessed now to inspire others to really find themselves and fulfil their own inner hunger. Everything I have done in my life has allowed and helped me to follow my purpose. From being a chef, running my business, my public speaking, the people I have encountered and all the lessons I have learned in the meantime.

So here we go. Let's start!

Love yourself
Loving yourself is no doubt the most important thing you can do for yourself, whatever is going on in your life, whatever you think you have done wrong or when you miss the love of others.

Love yourself; you are a divine being, here on your journey to learn and to remember. The love you are able to give to yourself will be reflected in equal amounts back to you. I can't tell you often enough about the importance of this.

It might seem at times that you are alone; always be good towards yourself and don't allow that little voice at any time to talk to you. Feel into your heart, as you start shining your light you will recognise the others around you doing the same, supporting and loving you.

Loving yourself first has nothing to do with being selfish. In an earlier chapter I wrote about giving and receiving and I described how we are always connected to the matrix, consciousness, the field, the life force, god, love, the universe or whatever you call it. You are always connected and you always receive. We live in abundance and remind yourself of this on a daily basis, as it will definitely help you in your growth and ongoing journeying.

Grounding
Ensure that you stay grounded all the time. It is easy to either get stuck and procrastinate or get this overwhelming feeling and praise yourself too much, the feeling that you are doing really well. Of course you are doing well, it is also important to find the balance between giving yourself too much praise and being consciously aware of what is going on, on a physical level.

Make sure you are grounded and stay real, see how the people closest to you respond to your journey, how they are feeling, and what is going on for them. Ground yourself in the sense that you check in on a regular basis on the progress you are making and how you are reacting to what is happening in your life and the life of others. One of the pitfalls which can overcome you and maybe allow you to be less grounded can be the ego, and more specifically the spiritual ego, this may happen to all of us at some stage. It is the point where we pride ourselves that we have done a lot already, that we are advanced and have quite some knowledge by now. The spiritual ego will close our eyes, believing we have done enough or are better than others, it might even tell us our thinking or beliefs are the best.

Be aware and always check in on yourself to see what is really happening.

There are various exercises you can do to ground yourself - cooling exercises a friend of mine always calls them. This can be walking in nature, some kind of yoga, or spending time with children and animals.

Journal
This is very important and something I recommend everyone to do, from people I mentor to the ones I meet for one-to-one sessions. Keep a

journal, write preferably on a daily basis but a least a few times a week. What has been happening for you? What were your challenges and how did you react, did you have any insights? Where did you feel you grew?

Any particular things which happened, stories which came back to you from when you were younger, how were your meditations. Wise things a friend said to you or what you learnt from a speaker at an event.

Write them down, and read them regularly, you will be surprised by the growth you experience and the coincidences which occur. I have kept all my journals for many years and love to look at them regularly, as there is so much I take away from them every time.

Keep your light alight
There is a light burning inside each of us, sometimes it feels like a little tea light and at other times it is like a wild burning campfire. Keep this light alight inside you all the time; even at the most challenging times ensure you connect with this light. You can do that, for example by thinking of all the things which make you come alive. This can be connected to playing with young children, seeing some friends, going on a small trip or having that coffee with your mum that you have been meaning to do.

It is important to keep that flame inside you burning, as at times we might feel it is gone, when you connect to it you will find it easier to overcome any challenge or difficult situation. As you shine your own light it is the only way to light up other people around you. When you shine your light it doesn't cost you any energy to light up others.

Keep shining!

"Being is effortless. Becoming takes effort." J. Krishnamurti

Being...
In a metaphysical sense it is important just to be, to live in the moment. To be actually means to be your true self completely. The next list of words are reminders of how to stay in that balanced and peaceful place of being.

- Be honest

Being honest and truthful all the time comes from speaking the truth from your heart, being free of all constraints. Being truthful and honest is liberating and will bring you back to your core.

It has nothing to do with hurting people, it has to do with talking from your heart, when you talk from your heart you will know how to say the right thing in every situation. The people around you will understand and be grateful. Trust follows truth, you will experience that the right opportunities and people will be magically attracted to you.

When we are not truthful in our lives about what we feel or see, a certain energy will be opened up affecting ourselves and the people around us. Make sure you are being honest and speak the truth all the time. This may be difficult, don't be hard on yourself, and try to get better and more pure as time progresses.

- Be childlike

Look at the world from a child's perspective, look at it in wonder, as if everything you experience is new. Be excited and open. If you don't know how to act, go to a playground and see how young children play with each other and how they interact with their surroundings and are fearless. We live in a wonderful world where there is still so much to discover. It is powerful to look at the things around you from that perspective rather than maybe taking it for granted.

Get some of the childlike energy back into your life and tune into it often!

- Be responsible

Being on your transformational journey brings a lot of responsibility. The responsibility to act properly and be just to everyone around you and every being on this planet, the responsibility to bring forth your purpose and role into this world. You are also still responsible as a human being here in the paradigm which we live; you must look after the tasks and obligations you have at this present moment. That can be in your job, your family, your business and society, take up your responsibilities.

Act responsibly with the words you use and as you are on your path honour the people who are maybe not as advanced as you yet. Be responsible in the way you interact with others.

- Be authentic

Being authentic means to be you, fully. To be truthful and honest, show up as yourself. It is different than being honest; it means to be authentic in everything you do, feel, say and how you act. Be congruent with yourself and share this authentically.

- Be present

Live in the present moment with your heart open. It is only the present moment which exists. Be present to whatever is, free of any constraints, thoughts or judgements you might have. Quieten your thinking, stop analysing, dividing and making distinctions, simply see that you are at the core, and accept all things and beings as part of the experience. It just is, that is all, neither good nor bad.

Be present to whatever is happening free from all your thoughts and you will be able to feel the energies which pass right through you.

"Whatever the present moment contains, accept it as if you had chosen it. Always work with it, not against it. Make it your friend and ally, not your enemy. This will miraculously transform your whole life." Eckhart Tolle

Your health

Just like an athlete who can only be at his peak when he trains properly and regularly and eats well to make sure he in the best form, it is as important for you to make sure you are healthy and fit.

The term 'a healthy mind in a healthy body' exists for a reason. Of course you can heal your body yourself, and the whole transformational journey is one of healing. It helps and benefits enormously when you have a healthy lifestyle making sure you eat well and exercise. The body, mind and spirit work together and they work better together when we assist them where we can. A healthy lifestyle and staying fit will help your soul and your transformational journey. It is as simple as that.

You need to do what your body tells you to do, what feels best.

Drink water

This might seem a logical one and we all have heard the benefits and facts for drinking water. The reason why I mention this here is because when you do all this emotional work on yourself, going deep inside, issues will come up, some of your patterns and beliefs that have been with you for a long time and they need to leave your body. Drinking lots of water helps for these energies and toxins to leave. Keep your body hydrated as it is hard work.

Observe - Sense - Trust

I like these three words and follow them, I can do it most of the time. In every situation, sit in that nothingness, and feel. Then observe what is really going on, allow the energy to present it to you. Sense to me is listening to your intuition and the right signs might be shown to you in various ways, an email, a feeling you have, something you see in a paper or a friend who mentions something to you. You will 'know' when you sit in that stillness which action to take, you know what the right thing is to do. Trust that whatever is given to you is the right thing to do and follow through on that feeling with complete trust. Once you have made a decision, go for it, don't let your ego or limited belief system or anyone else stop you.

When you follow these three in the right order - observe, sense, trust - then you will do the right thing and find what you need on your way.

Who am I
As I was writing this chapter I was thinking back to the days when I used to be a chef. As conscious human beings we constantly work on ourselves and remove all impurities. The saucier is the alchemist of the kitchen, the person not only responsible for all sauces, also for the basis of these: the stocks. Stocks are the flavours extracted from the slow cooking of meat, fish bones or vegetables and herbs. When a stock is simmering away on the stove it is the saucier's job to remove all impurities from the liquid so the end result will be a clean-tasting and pure delicious sauce. This wouldn't happen if he didn't constantly remove all impurities which float to the surface. It is a labour-intensive job. Just as it is for our personal purification, you need to keep working on it.

In every stage of your journey and in your life, wherever you find yourself, check in with yourself and ask the questions: Who am I in this, am I being myself? Can I express myself fully, am I following my heart? Is this who I truly am?

When the answer to any these questions is no, or is an answer where you can't be yourself fully, it means that you have to make changes. Maybe even leave the situation, job, relationship or meeting. It is important that you are always true to yourself, stay in your core, on your path. The more you get off track the more difficult it will be to come back on course again.

Staying in your core will mean that you are in a stable vibration and the stillness will give you lots of choice. When you leave your centre the vibration will immediately be less stable, meaning you have less choice and balance and harmony will be more difficult to find.

Check in with yourself on a regular basis.

Your vibrational energy

We all have a certain energy on which we vibrate and that vibration gives us our uniqueness. Five thousand years ago, the I Ching, the Chinese book of wisdom, was written. For thousands of years the Chinese studied nature and understood that there is a cycle to everything. For example the seasons, they always go in a certain order, they never change. Winter, spring, summer, late summer and fall. These seasons have a certain energy as well as water, wood, fire, earth and metal. We each have a unique blend of these five energies and it really helps when you find out and understand your own unique energies.

We can talk about this for hours, however that is not the purpose of this book. Go to this website: https: www.fiveinstitute.com/take-the-vitality-test/ and take the free test. You will receive lots of information and be surprised how accurate it is and most of all, it is fun. It will not only help you to understand yourself better, it will help you to understand better why you do things in a certain way and why some things always seem to fail or are more challenging for you.

After a bit of practice you also get to understand the energy patterns and behaviours of others.

Understand your vibration.

Meditation

There are many ways and courses on how to meditate. The most important is to develop a habit of regular meditation. You will be guided to what is best for you, find a quiet place to do it and meditate at regular times. Just like exercise you will become dependent on it. Besides finding the stillness and peace within yourself, it is also the place and moment to talk to your guides, to ask for help, guidance and advice.

Some years ago I was taught a visioning meditation. This particular one is used by athletes to vision the race they are going to run or drive. I have used it to create a whole new world, where I spend much of my time and where I connect with other beings for my guidance.

Find a quiet place where you won't be disturbed.

Make yourself comfortable in your chair, place your feet firmly on the ground and keep your back straight.

Close your eyes and go to that place where you were happiest as a child when you were eleven years old. All of a sudden you see a small door somewhere which you have never seen before. You are curious and you go through that door.

As you enter the new space everything turns red, and slowly from red everything turns orange, then yellow and the yellow slowly turns into a beautiful vibrant green. The green then turns into blue and as the blue fades everything becomes indigo. You now see that the indigo almost unnoticeably has turned in a violet colour. In the distance you see a set of stairs which bask in white light, and as you are curious you go up the stairs set in this beautiful white light.

There are ten steps and you count slowly as you go up the stairs, taking one step at a time.

On the top of the stairs you see a door, now look at the door. Notice which material it is made of, how big is it, is it heavy? You get hold of the door now, how does it feel, is it cold, warm or do you notice the carving in the wood?

As you enter the door there are people to greet you, they are happy to see you. Say hello to them in your own way. On your right hand side there is another door, go through that door and there is a desk with a chair. As you sit down, a computer screen pops up. What is on that screen? There are magazines lying around, what do you see on the front covers? Are they giving you a message?

On the left hand side is a beautiful couch overlooking the ocean. You discover that there is another door which leads to a few stairs into a boardroom. Here you can come to ask questions to anyone, think of people and souls you admire, invite them into the boardroom. Who is showing up? Have a conversation with them, ask them the questions you like to ask.

Leave them now with your questions and go back in 1-2 days to hear the answers. Leave the boardroom and wander around; what other rooms do you detect, is there a garden? What is happening?

When you are ready, go back to the entrance, say goodbye to everyone and tell them you will be back. Slowly go down the ten stairs and then go down the colours in reverse order: violet, indigo, blue, green, yellow, orange and red, as you have done so bring your awareness back to the room where you are in and open your eyes slowly and take a couple of deep breaths.

This is a powerful visualisation – meditation method which you can use to create everything. I call it my workshop and have created my house, book and foundation in that space. You can create the different rooms, garden and house there exactly as you want it. The more you go back and tune in and connect the more you will get the answers and visions you are looking for.

> "As I walked toward the gate that would lead to my freedom, I knew if I didn't leave my bitterness and hatred behind, I'd still be in prison."
> Nelson Mandela

Have a mentor

Make sure you have a mentor to support you at every stage of your journey; someone who has done it before, who is usually two steps ahead of you, so they can guide you and advise you as they can see clearly what is going on for you before you are aware of it yourself.

Honour these people as it will make your transformation easier. More importantly they can help you to make sense of occurrences when you can't yourself. Mentors are important to have in your business and career. Good chefs always have a mentor, often a top chef they worked for. You can even have different mentors at the same time for different areas in your life. Richard Branson is well known for saying that he has five mentors at any given moment in his life.

Ensure you have the right people around you and you learn from their experience and wisdom. For the transformational journey look at people with balance, wisdom and peace within themselves.

Connect the dots

Connecting the dots can only be done backwards, however when do we take the time to do this? Who takes the time to look at the significant moments in their lives from the perspective of stillness? The dots tell you everything you need to know really about your life's purpose and the journey you experience. Set the time aside on a regular basis, write the significant dots down and discover the connections and understand what they are telling you on a deeper level.

Be honest and precise to yourself and let yourself be guided by the understanding flow about the next step. As you become more aware of the significant moments in your life, you will also be more aware when these significant moments occur in the present moment and what they mean for you.

I call it drawing by numbers which I loved as a child. At first the dots meant nothing, then slowly as the picture became clearer you could start to see the end result and you got more excited and wanted to finish it. Life is exactly the same.

Get excited again!

> "There is a growing body of anecdotal evidence, combined with solid research efforts, that suggests intuition is a critical aspect of how we humans interact with our environment and how, ultimately, we make many of our decisions," Ivy Estabrooke

Rite of passage
A rite of passage, sometimes called initiation, is a ritual event that marks a person's transition from one status to another. It is still used in many indigenous cultures and often marks the event from a boy to becoming a man, or from girl to woman. It is like cutting the umbilical cord. Young men and women had to perform certain tasks to prove that they were ready to become a woman or a man.

We have lost this in our modern culture and the reason many males and females are still struggling with part of their identity is because they don't know what it truly means to be a woman or man in their society. We have not just lost the rituals often the right role models are lacking in our lives, the people we look up to, or can go to for advice to show us how things are done.

When you are on your journey and discovering who you truly are, keep this in mind. Some of your challenges might come from the fact that you never felt you were shown how to be a mum or how to be a woman in a male-dominated society. This can have huge impacts on our struggle and the related belief systems.

Girls were initiated as women and in the indigenous villages the women would come together and talk about all kinds of issues. The girls than felt part of a group, and the same goes for boys of course. We often miss that belonging, being part of a peer group where we are truly a part of a safe environment in which to talk, share and get advice. It is important for both men and women to have these groups where we can go to for advice, guidance or just a chat. To belong and feel a part of it, and most importantly that we feel that we are a good husband, wife, woman, partner, mother or father. There is a lot of uncertainty about these issues and we are never shown how to do these roles right; the uncertainty brings a lot of unnecessary fear and worry.

> "Move like a beam of light,
> Fly like lightning,
> Strike like thunder,
> Whirl in circles around a stable center."
> Morihei Ueshiba

Inner hunger
Hunger means longing for, and we all long for something; love, wealth, connection, understanding or just friendship. Loneliness is the biggest challenge we face in our Western world. Always check in with yourself and ask: what am I hungry for? What am I longing for right now in this moment?

The answers can be very revealing and will help you with the issues and challenges which come up. You might be hungry for friendship as you feel lonely. When you don't address that you may notice that you look at friendships and meetings from that perspective. Your hunger or loneliness might cause you to think that people don't make time for you, or don't like you or you might even have the feeling that you are not important enough.

Always address that hunger, begin to understand where your hunger is coming from, what is the core issue underlying it? It is most likely something which happened in the past. Go to the core of it and work on it to let it go. Once you have tackled the core issue underlying your hunger, the issue will disappear in the present time as well.

So what are you hungry for? Not a sandwich, pizza or just something sweet? Tune in and check why you have certain feelings when you get triggered.

Share your gift
We all have a unique gift to share with the world. Your gift is so obvious and yet you may not notice it; it is such an integral part of you that it is effortless to you. Many of us don't even realise our gift. Sometimes we don't even notice we are sharing it, and that it is of huge value to others.

The value of everyone's gift is equally important. In the way we live our lives currently and the way we have built our economy, it is something we have forgotten. Certain gifts have become of greater perceived value because they can be sold for money. Think of talented singers, star football players and other obvious skills that are monetised in our economy. Society conditions us to believe that these are the more valuable gifts, and people with these gifts receive larger sums of money than others with maybe less obvious gifts.

Share your gift freely with the world as this opens up energy, when you open up one energy field, the energy opens somewhere else as well, it is one of the basic laws of the universe - don't hold back!

Here is an exercise to discover your gift in 15 minutes. You just need a friend to help you. Enjoy!

Make yourselves comfortable and sit very close to each other. Put your left hand on the other person's right shoulder so that a circle is created by your arms. This is a circle of trust. Decide who goes first and that person tells the other one what their gift is.

Take 5 minutes to do this part and be very specific. Give clear examples. Also share situations when your gift didn't serve you well, when you were challenged. The other person just listens. If you don't know what your gift is, just start talking, intuitively it will come to you.

I normally experience that people can't stop talking after 5 minutes.

After 5 minutes the person who listened, shares what they've heard and what they feel the gift is. Repeat what you believe the first person's gift means to the world. Not just what the first person said, also share what intuitively came to you as a listener.

Take 2-3 minutes to do this. The first person just listens and takes it all in. Repeat the exercise in reverse order and be amazed at what you learn about yourself.

> "Your soul doesn't care what you do for a living - and when your life is over, neither will you. Your soul cares only about what you are being while you are doing whatever you are doing."
> Neale Donald Walsch

Contribution

Start to contribute to your community, to a charity, to neighbours or someone in need immediately. We often hear that people start giving back or helping when they have their own life sorted, when they have enough money in the bank. We are here to share our gifts freely for the greater good, if you don't do that than you block the flow of energy. Not just your own, also that of the people around you and humanity in general.

Have a look around you, see what kind of help you would like to offer and where you can help. Even if there is not a lot of time at the moment, start for example by helping elderly in your local community even when it is an hour a week. Maybe you can make a website for free for a charity, offering your expertise.

What it does is that it will change your mind-set. In one of the earlier chapters I explained about giving and receiving. Giving is all we have! Start giving as you are already connected to the abundance. Tune in constantly and see if you are giving enough.

Contribute to what is closest to your heart and your purpose; as you do so you will experience many other fields in your life opening up magically. Give back!

Alchemy menu
At the end of this book I thought about giving you a menu. Sometimes you hear the question, what would your last meal be? I always call it my desert island dish. I have created here a menu with dishes I really like and which is put together in line with the steps we have taken in this book.

You can find the recipes on the website www.insideoutbook.me/recipe

Crushed raw vegetable salad
The best raw vegetables in a dressing with peanuts and lime.

Laksa
Spicy Malaysian soup with coconut cream and langoustines.

Lobster Marie Louise
Grilled lobster with garlic and a tomato and tarragon Béarnaise sauce.

Pot au Feu
A selection of meats slow-cooked in bouillon with condiments.

Cheese
A selection of fine cheese and breads.

Whole roasted pine apple
Pineapple, vanilla, rum, caramel, mango and chilli ice cream.

ABOUT LEON

I was born the eldest of four children in a loving family near Maastricht in the Netherlands, where my parents ran their own business. When I was eight years old I had many friends and I was doing really well at school, never one of the best, just a little bit behind them.

One day when playing football, two of my best friends took turns in choosing their team. You must understand that I couldn't play football for my life. My friends picked boys we didn't like before me, and at the time that did hurt me quite a bit, I couldn't understand how they would choose these boys over me. We were best friends? My friends just wanted to win the match. They didn't relate it to our friendship; I did!

That day as a young boy I made the conscious decision to prove that I could be number one in something, and subconsciously I was looking for that opportunity all the time. Being number one became the driving force in my life, it also drove me away further from my core, away from the person who I truly am.

Through this drive I had become one of the best chefs of my generation in the Netherlands. After I proved I could excel as a chef at the highest level I needed a new fix, I moved to London to start a fine food wholesale business to prove that I am a good businessman.

Just a few years ago I finally managed to break this pattern, which was like a new beginning, a rebirth. It happened during an entrepreneurs business masters' programme – EBS - in Bali in 2007. Seven international mentors during an eight-day programme transformed twelve business people from all over the world. At the time I was running my food wholesale business in London. We were very successful, it did however cost me all my energy to succeed as I always felt uncomfortable with the way we did business with each other. It was just about money. All my life I thought it was just me. Intuitively, it always felt 'wrong'; it seemed to me that I was the only one.

During that week in Bali, I made a very conscious decision to stop and quit my business. I had enough. It was time for time for me to follow my own path again, and to rediscover who I truly am.

It was one of those courses where you have to present a plan, the mentors first totally break it down, all controlled of course in order for you to come out better, clearer and wiser in the end. To build you up again. During that week I was asked a few times, "Leon, tell us your story again!" They loved it, that I had been a top chef in Holland who started a business out of nothing in London and now had some ideas to run an international social enterprise. This, however, was not the way I took it. When asked: who are you? I started pondering, yes, who am I? Everyone thought I was very successful, I only saw the challenges, which was all I could see going on. I realised I was very successful but that was only on the outside. That success didn't make me happy on the inside. I had a deep emotional drive to achieve everything I did; that came from my feeling that I was not good enough and the need to always prove myself.

Asking myself truthfully: who are you? The deep insights it gave me at the time, made me decide to stop my wholesale business on my return to London. Not to sell it. We closed it. Within just six short weeks! It was the best decision I've ever made. I was free. Now I could be truly me and not 'pretend' to be what the world wanted me to be. Potentially I said goodbye to a lot of money, I have never been money-driven, I was just so ready to stop as I realised it wasn't me. I had nothing to prove.

The deep realisation was that although I was successful on the outside, I was very unhappy on the inside. The signs had been there for a while, which is why I had so many challenges. The universe was giving me all the signs. It wasn't my purpose anymore. I couldn't be part of a world which I didn't support and I knew I needed to change.

On the plane back from Bali to London, I made the conscious decision to follow my heart. It was the longest flight ever due to delays, the result of this deep change was that suddenly my life started flowing again. In the months afterwards, I rediscovered my innate purpose, started my charity and wrote a book. Only because I did the necessary work on myself, my heart opened and I regained and followed that inner 'knowing.'

I started on the journey of turning myself inside out, I share this story with you in this book and show you how you can open your heart and become who you truly are free of all constraints. Nothing has more power than being your true self, to be who you truly are and live from your most inner core being.

That is the most powerful gift you can give yourself and the world around you. Who doesn't sometimes have the feeling of Is this it? Surely there should be more to life? Life should be more than a daily cycle of eat, sleep, drink, and a party at the weekend?

When you have that feeling sometimes, then join us and your life will be transformed.

Happiness is an inside job. You can only change the outside world when you change your inside first. As within, so without!

"Twenty years from now you will be more disappointed by the things that you didn't do than by the ones you did do, so throw off the bowlines, sail away from safe harbour, and catch the trade winds in your sails. Explore, Dream, Discover." Mark Twain

Other Books by Leon

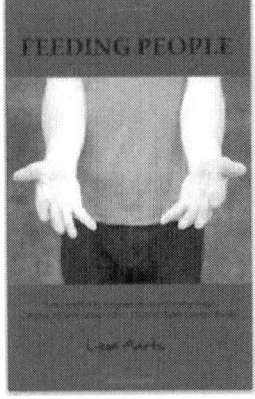

What if it actually is simple to do great things, and to leave a lasting legacy? The author is a social entrepreneur, dad, chef, philanthropist, traveller and founder of Extraordinary Ones. In this book, he shows us what happens when we all become truly connected to each other again and with ourselves, we make a huge difference.

Who doesn't want to be in love all the time? Most of us know that feeling of being in love... you can feel your heart beat in your throat, you always feel very nice and warm and you have that nice, slightly nauseating feeling in your heart. Now isn't that just the greatest feeling to be in love? When you are in love you will do anything to be with your loved one

I have collected some of the recipes from my earlier career as a chef for you, as a little token for you to enjoy and to explore the connection between Alchemy and cooking. I still use many of these recipes at home and when I cook for friends.

Visit http://tinyurl.com/k5ocfdh to purchase these and other books by Leon.

Made in the USA
Charleston, SC
28 February 2016